GOLF MADE SIMPLE

Second Edition

William R. Lamb

D1604821

KENDALL/HUNT PUBLISHING COMPANY
4050 Westmark Drive   Dubuque, Iowa 52002

CONTENTS

PREFACE

Golf is truly a lifetime sport and a wonderful game. It challenges us, both mentally and physically, and serves as a great way to relieve stress amongst some of the most beautiful scenery one can imagine. Golf is more than a game; it's a journey. Along the way we develop life long friendships, learn much about responsibility, commitment, the benefits of hard work, and more than anything else, ourselves. The game can and should provide each of us with a lifetime full of enjoyment.

Although golf is perhaps the fastest growing sport in the world, many take up the game and then quit shortly thereafter. Frustration is perhaps the biggest culprit behind this quick exodus. Golf can be tremendously frustrating to a beginner, especially one who tries to take on the challenge alone. There certainly is enough material available for the beginner who wishes to teach himself; however, the information can be quite confusing and simply make matters worse.

The purpose of this book is to provide beginners, intermediate players, and advanced players with the simple fundamentals necessary to play the game of golf. It also provides students with a much-needed look at others areas of the game. Understanding terminology, the history, learning good etiquette, the basic rules, scoring, and a little about equipment is instrumental in becoming a good golfer. This book addresses both the mental and physical aspects of the game, the right and wrong way to practice, the short game, trouble shots and yes, even how to swing a golf club.

The golf swing is simple, often times difficult only due to a lack of understanding. There are literally thousands of books and tapes developed each year to help people play better golf and yet the national average handicap for a male is within a stroke of what it was 30 years ago. In spite of all the advances in equipment we have not improved. The reason is simply, there is no secret swing or method that's going to help you play better. You must develop good fundamentals. Every swing fault is a result of poor fundamentals. With good fundamentals and practice anyone can learn to play and enjoy this game. Hopefully this book will make the learning process easier, the game more fun, and send you on your way to a lifetime of enjoyment—good luck and play well.

William R. Lamb

ACKNOWLEDGMENTS

Writing this book was much more work than I had anticipated. It has been, however, a wonderful experience. To say the least my typing skills have improved. I'm now using three fingers and probably reaching speeds of say perhaps 10-12 words per minute. I would like to thank Dr. Dick Couey, not only for his input but especially his guidance and support along the way. A special thanks to Adam Meyer and the rest of my students for allowing me to use their images as well as continuing to make me look like a great teacher. I'd like to thank Dr. Cook and the Mindset Academy for allowing me to share his teachings. And last but not least, I'd like to thank my family, my wife Cheryl, my sons Shannon, Nicholus, and Trevor for supporting me in this endeavor. Oh yea my dog Hogan for not eating the final copy when he had a chance to do so.

GOLF: TRULY A LIFETIME SPORT

Golf: Truly a Lifetime Sport

Golf is an intelligent game played by intelligent people but not always in an intelligent way. Those of you who play golf have little trouble relating to this statement. More often than not golfers find themselves looking back on a particular shot or hole during a round of golf and wondering if perhaps they had been possessed by a demon that clearly had never played the game before. Everyone who plays the game makes mistakes; those who make the fewest play the best. Most mistakes made on the course are mental. Many golfers try to accomplish in one shot what clearly requires two shots and in doing so inevitably take three shots. Yoggi Berra once commented about golf mental errors as, "golf is <u>90%</u> mental and the other half is skill." Swing faults are not mistakes; they are simply a result of a lack of experience or a lack of preparation. This book will teach you the rules and etiquette as well as help you develop good swing fundamentals and make fewer mental errors, thus allowing you to play better golf and enjoy this fascinating game. Let's start by examining some of golf's intriguing history.

History of the Game

Although the roots of golf are not totally clear it is believed the game originated in Scotland. Scottish Shepards, using their crooks to knock pebbles into small holes in the ground thousands of years ago, are credited with being the first to play. Others believe that the game began in Holland. Legend has it that mentally ill patients who were institutional-ized in Holland were given sticks to knock around small rocks during their time outside.

This kept them busy and provided them with exercise. While trading with Scotland across the English Channel, Hollanders would show the Scots this game and then quietly make fun of the Scotts for acting like the mentally ill patients back home. Being mentally ill is not a pre requisite for playing golf; however at times it can be considered an asset. The first documented evidence of the game in Scotland was in the 15th century. King James the II prohibited golf because it detracted from the skill of archery, and at that time the defense of the country depended greatly upon expertise with bow and arrow. King James the IV descended to the throne in 1500 and became interested in the game and soon opposition disappeared. Mary, Queen of Scots, is thought to be the first woman to play the game.

Over the ensuing years many golf organizations and groups began to appear. Golf as a sport evolved in the mid 18th century when the St. Andrews Society of Golfers was formed and the first rules were written. Those 13 rules are still the nucleus of the rules we use today. In 1884 the Society became the famous Royal and Ancient Golf Club of St. Andrews. The course at St. Andrews originally had 22 holes but was later shortened to 18.

The first tournament played was the British Open held in 1860 at the St. Andrews course. The open is still played today and is designated as one of the 4 major championships on the PGA tour. The others are the Masters, the US Open, and the PGA Championship. Twenty-five years after the first British Open tournament was held, the first British amateur championship was completed.

Bobby Jones
(Photo courtesy of USGA.
All Rights Reserved.)

A Scot named John Ried introduced golf to the United States in 1888. Ried and his neighbors played the game on a 3-hole course and shared a single set of clubs. The first recognized golf course to be built was in Yonkers, New York in 1888. Four years later Shinnecock Hills, also in New York, was built and became the first organized golf club in the US as well as the first to build a clubhouse. Golf historians are unclear as to where the first 18-hole course was built in the US. It is believed that the Chicago Club in Illinois may have been the first to be built when Blair McDonald, an American who went to school in Scotland, enlarged the club from 9 to 18 holes in the late 19th century. The game began to grow and the first public golf links were built in New York City just before the turn of the century. From that time forward golf became a sport available to all classes of people, although early on it was enjoyed by mostly the wealthy.

Francis Quimet
(Photo courtesy of USGA.
All Rights Reserved.)

The USGA (United States Golf Association) was formed in1895. Its purpose was to serve as the official caretaker of the game. Responsibilities included growing the game, testing and controlling new equipment, enforcing and revising the rules as well as insuring the integrity of the sport. That same year the USGA conducted 3 tournaments, the US Amateur, the US Open for men, and the US Open for women. It took 16 years for an American to win the US Open. In 1911 Johnny McDermott became the first to do so. Two years later in 1913 Francis Quimet became the first American amateur to win the Open tournament. Later a great amateur golfer from Georgia named Bobby Jones won all four major tournaments in one year, (the British Open, the British Amateur, as well as the US Open and the US Amateur), a feat that to this day has not been equaled.

Golf is much the same game today as it was in Europe 500 years ago. The game grew at a relatively steady pace after its introduction into the United States until late in the 1950's when its popularity increased greatly. Players like Arnold Palmer and Jack Nicklaus caused increased television coverage, which introduced many new people to the game. In recent years, however, players such as Tiger Woods have made golf even more popular and with a much more diversified group of people. Golf today is perhaps the fastest growing sport in the world with more than 25 million people playing in the United States alone. Golf courses are found everywhere in the US today. Not only large cities but also even the smallest of

Trevor Lamb's golf swing at age 9, front and back views.

towns usually have their own golf courses. It is a game enjoyed by both young and old, male and female and is considered to be a sport one can enjoy for a lifetime.

The Game Today

A friend of mine once commented, "Golf is not a matter of life and death; it's more serious than that". Golf is more than just a game; it's a journey. Along the way we develop life long friendships, learn much about responsibility, commitment, the benefits of hard work, and more than anything else, ourselves. Shivas Irons, a Scottish golf professional once said, "Nowhere does a man go so naked as on a golf course". You can tell a lot about a person's life by the way he or she plays golf. **There is a right speed for playing the game, as there is a right speed for living one's life.**

Some say golf is perhaps the greatest game man ever invented. The uniqueness of the game of golf is unparalleled by any sport in that individuals of all ages and skill levels can compete head to head due to its handicapping system. Golf is more than just a game that challenges us; it's an excellent means of exercise both, physically and mentally, and it provides a great avenue to relieve stress, or at least it used to.

Today's fast paced society, however, has taken some of the enjoyment and many of the benefits away from the game. What was once an enjoyable walk through some of the most spectacular landscaping one could imagine is now a motorized race from one tee to eighteen green. Modern scenery includes signs informing you how many holes you should have completed in a given time, a Marshall watching your every move to insure you will set a new course record for speed of play, and numerous individuals shouting and hitting shots past you to let you know "light speed" is not fast enough.

The problem cannot be blamed on any one culprit but several. As mentioned before, golf is one of the fastest growing sports today. Over twenty-five million people play in the United States alone. Facilities are expensive to build and even more expensive to maintain. A facility must run as many people through its doors per day as possible in an attempt to stay open. All this combined with the fact people have poor time management skills and are usually rushed from morning to night seem to have made golf less the game it was. Hopefully this book will help you not only learn to play better golf but also learn to enjoy the game the way it was meant to be enjoyed.

Benefits of Playing Golf

The benefits of playing the game of golf are many. One of the great things about golf is that for the most part it can be enjoyed year round except in the northernmost states in the US. It is a game that can be played by yourself or with a group of friends, a game that allows grandfathers to play with their grandsons and husbands to play with their wives, (not recommended). It's a game that allows players of different levels to compete with each other on

The physical benefits of playing golf are extremely good especially if you walk. Research has shown that walking a mile with a 20-pound golf bag burns approximately 150 calories. Most golf courses are four to five miles in length, depending on the length between holes. The normal golfer will burn approximately 750 to 900 calories, depending on his/her ability, or about 7 to 10 calories a shot. This would indicate that unskilled golfers burn more calories than skilled golfers. Unskilled golfers thus have a positive rationalization for playing golf; they can lose more weight.

the same playing field due to its unique handicap system. It is without a doubt the game of a lifetime.

Walking and carrying your bag as opposed to riding a golf cart is highly recommended. Although golf carts do serve a very important purpose, allowing those who are physically challenged due to age or handicaps to continue to play, walking is great for your cardiovascular system as well as excellent for toning the different muscle groups. Research has shown that walking a 15-minute mile burns 100 calories, while running a 6-minute mile burns 108 calories. So why lose your dinner for 8 calories; slow down and enjoy the scenery.

Also of great importance are the mental benefits of playing the game. In our fast paced society golf offers us a chance to relax and unwind amongst some of the most beautiful scenery in the world. Mark Twain once said, "golf is a good walk spoiled", and if you forget that golf is just a game that can be somewhat true. However, if you can learn to leave the world behind and focus on the task at hand you will find golf can be mentally challenging in a positive way. To play well you must think your way around the course, playing to your strengths and away from your weaknesses. The feeling one experiences when pulling off that one great shot or reaching his target score for the first time is indescribable and does wonders for one's well being.

As a PGA teaching professional I spend the majority of my time teaching people to play golf. My youngest student is 2 and my oldest is 91. I teach men and women alike as well as amateurs (golfers who play and compete for fun) and professionals (golfers who play and compete for money).
Golf truly is a lifetime sport. Below are a few helpful hints to those of you who are just beginning to play.

A Game for Everyone

Golf used to be referred to as a rich man's game, and for the most part was only enjoyed by those that were financially well off. Over the years that has changed drastically and people from all walks of life, regardless of their race, color, or creed enjoy golf. There are no prerequisites for those who wish to play the game. One can be short or tall, slow or fast, intelligent or not so intelligent, and even handicapped and still enjoy the game of golf. I've had students as young as age two and as old as age 87.

Play during Non Peak Hours

Ask your local professional when his facility is the least congested and try to play during those times. Usually this will be early morning or late afternoon, both of which many of us prefer. Late afternoon is especially nice since it's usually cooler and one can walk and not be rushed. You may only be able to complete nine holes, but it will be an enjoyable nine holes. Try to avoid a weekend if possible; that is when most courses do the majority of their business.

Walk Whenever Possible

You will find you play much better when you walk. It gives you time to think between shots and enjoy your surroundings as well as much needed exercise.

Don't Dwell On Your Score

It is important to realize that one's score is not an exact mirror of one's worth. Graciously accept your place on the golfing ladder. If you are not satisfied with how well you play, take a few golf lessons from your local PGA professional.

Enjoy the Game

Never forget that golf is a game. No one has ever mastered the game and no one ever will. Allow yourself to be challenged but not overwhelmed. In golf as in life things that seem of great importance one day matter not the next. Enjoy the game, enjoy the learning process, and enjoy the challenges put before you. Golf is a journey unlike any other except perhaps that of life. Some days are better than others; just remember the bad days serve a valuable purpose. To truly appreciate success you must experience a taste of failure. Enjoy the game and the journey.

Name _____   Section _____

Chapter One Review

1. When was golf introduced into the United States? _____

2. Where was the first tournament held and in what year?

    _____

3. What does the USGA stand for? _____

4. What are the responsibilities of the USGA?

    _____

    _____

5. What club became the first organized golf club in the US?

    _____

6. Approximately how many people play golf in the US? _____

7. Who was the first American to win the US Open? _____

8. List two benefits of playing golf.

    _____

9. Approximately how many calories does one burn per shot while playing golf?

    _____

10. How might learning to play golf benefit you?

    _____

11. What's the single most important thing to remember about the game of golf?

    _____

    Why are you taking this class?

    _____

    _____

    List 4 goals you would like to accomplish by the end of this class.

    a. _____

    b. _____

    c. _____

    d. _____

CHAPTER TWO

HOW THE GAME IS PLAYED

Course Layout and Terminology

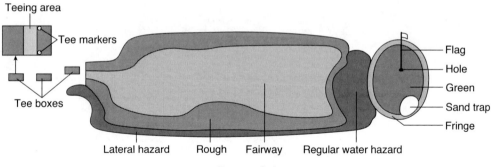

Figure 2.1

Tee Box	Area from which you are required to begin play on each hole.
Tee Markers	Markers on tee box that define front boundaries of teeing area.
Teeing Area	Rectangular area in which the ball must be teed to begin play on each hole. The area is defined by drawing a line between the tee markers and another two club lengths back.
Fairway	Closely mown area between the tee and the green.
Rough	Area that borders fairway, the grass is cut slightly higher than the fairway.
Green	Putting surface, which contains the hole. The grass is cut lower than the fairway.
Hole	Hole in the green in which the ball must come to rest.
Flag	Pole with flag that identifies where the hole is located on the green.

Fringe	Closely mown area around the green. The grass is cut lower than the fairway but not as low as the green.
Cup	Metal or plastic cup placed inside the hole to hold the flag.
Lateral Hazard	Area on the course filled with water. Lateral hazards are defined by **red** lines or stake.
Regular Hazard	Area on the course filled with water. Regular hazards are defined by **yellow** lines or stake.
Sand Trap	Area on the course that is filled with sand and serves as an obstacle.

Swing Terms

Setup	The way we position ourselves to the ball.
Balance	Ability to transfer weight smoothly throughout the golf swing.
Swing Plane	Path that the club travels around the body.
Flat	Shallow swing plane
Upright	Upright swing plane
Laid off	Club points to left of target line at the top of the swing (for right handed golfers).
Down the line	Club points parallel to the target line at the top of the swing (for right handed golfers).
Across the line	Club points to right of target line at the top of the swing (for right handed golfers).
Grip	The way the hands are positioned on the golf club.
Weak	Both hands turned to the left (for right handed golfers).
Strong	Both hands turned to the right (for right handed golfers).
Neutral	Hands in more of a palm-facing-palm position.
Clubface	Front portion of the club head, which contacts the ball.
Square	The clubface is aimed directly at the target.
Opened	The clubface is aimed right of the target (for right handed golfers).
Closed	The clubface is aimed left of the target (for right handed golfers).
Alignment	The way the body is positioned in relationship to the target.
Open	Shoulders, hips, and feet are aligned left of the target line (for right handed golfers).
Closed	Shoulders, hips, and feet are aligned right of the target line (for right handed golfers).
Square	Shoulders, hips, and feet are aligned parallel to the target line.

Club terms

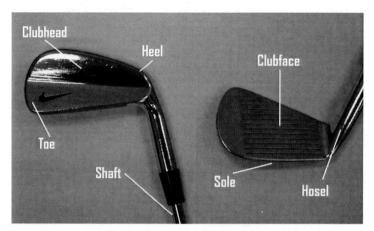

Figure 2.2

Object of the Game

The object of the game at first glance seems relatively simple. All one has to do is to hit a 1.61 inch diameter ball into a 4.25 inch diameter hole in as few swings as possible. This is, however, where the simplicity ends. The reality is that the game is much more complicated than just hitting a ball into a hole. One has to take in to account the speed and direction of wind, the undulations of the fairway and greens, he must avoid sand traps, trees, high rough, water hazards, and out-of-bounds, in order to be successful at golf. Winston Churchill describes the objective of golf as " a game whose aim is to hit a very small ball into a very small hole, with weapons singularly ill-designed for the purpose". Hopefully, the following paragraphs will give you a better understanding of how the game is played.

There is a starting point referred to as the **tee box.** On the tee box there is a specific area you must begin play from. This area is called the **teeing area.** (See figure 2.1) The teeing area is defined by drawing an imaginary line between the **tee markers.** Tee markers identify the position on the tee box from which you must hit your tee shot. Another imaginary line that is defined by the length of two golf clubs extends backwards from the tee markers. You must tee your ball up within this imaginary rectangular area; however, you may stand outside of the area as long as your golf ball is within the area. You may place the ball on the ground or you can place it on a tee, which is a small peg designed to hold the ball above the ground.

There are several sets of tee boxes on each hole. The set farthest from the hole are the most challenging and are usually referred to as the professional tees. The next teeing area is closer to the hole and is slightly less challenging. This set is usually referred to as the men's tees. The tees closest to the green are the least challenging and are referred to as the ladies' tees. A better way of defining the tees would be to call them the beginner, the intermediate, and the advanced tees. **If you are a beginner, man or woman, you should start playing at the front tees. As your skill level increases then you should move back to a tee that challenges you.**

Between the Tee box and the **green** (putting surface which contains the hole) is the **fairway.** The fairway is a closely mown area in which you try to make your ball come to rest on your way to the green. An area of grass that is much longer surrounds the fairway and is referred to as the **rough.** The rough is much harder to play a shot from and should be avoided if at all possible. Throughout the fairway and the rough are areas known as **hazards.** Hazards are obstacles put there that add beauty as well as to make the game more challenging. Hazards may be in the form of **water hazards** (areas filled with water) or in the form of **sand traps** (areas filled with sand). (See figure 2.1) There are specific rules that apply when playing out of these hazards. These rules will be discussed in the rules section of this book.

After you have hit your ball from the teeing area, hopefully into the fairway and not into the rough or hazards and have reached the green, you will find a 4.25-inch diameter metal or plastic cup placed six inches deep into the putting surface. A flag on a pole is placed in the cup so it can be seen from a distance. An area of grass, known as the **fringe,** surrounds the green and helps to separate the green from the fairway. When your ball comes to rest on the green you may pick it up for the first time since hitting it from the tee box. Never pick your ball up until it comes to rest on the putting surface unless local rules specify otherwise. Before picking the ball up you must mark where it lies accurately so that it may be replaced when it is your turn to play. When your ball is farthest from the cup you are said to be **away** and must try to hit the ball into the hole in as few strokes as possible. The club of choice should be the putter; however, you may use any club in your bag.

Your score is simply the summation of the number of strokes it took you to get your ball from the tee to the hole and includes any misses and or penalty shots. After you have finished the first hole, you may proceed to the second hole. Upon finishing eighteen holes, the summation of the strokes on each hole will determine your score.

The Equipment

The equipment we use to play the game consists of a set of golf clubs (irons and woods), a putter, balls, tees, a glove, shoes, and a bag to carry all of it. During a round of golf you may use any club for any shot that you may encounter. Sometimes this is a bit of a problem since you are allowed to carry 14 clubs in your bag. To choose the right club for a particular shot requires one to have an understanding of the clubs and their playing characteristics. Each club varies in length and in the amount of loft on the clubface. These two features, along with club head speed, are what determine how high or low and how far the ball will travel. The following pictures show how the lengths of the clubs and lofts vary. (See figure 2.3)

As the length of the club gets shorter, the loft of the clubface increases. (See figure 2.4a and 2.4b) The result is that the shorter the iron the higher and shorter the ball will travel. The ball will travel higher due to the increased loft and will travel a shorter distance because less club head speed is generated with the shorter shaft.

A normal set of clubs includes a couple of woods, some irons and a putter. **The longer the iron the smaller the number on the iron will be.** A 2-iron, for example, is longer than a 7-iron. The same holds true with the woods. A typical set will include: a number 1-wood, 3-wood, (hybrid), 3-iron thru 9-iron, a pitching wedge, a sand wedge, a lob wedge, and a putter (see figure 2.4c). The putter has little or no loft and is used to roll the ball into the hole once you have reached the green. The 2, 3, and 4-irons are referred to as the **long irons**. The 5, 6, and 7 irons are referred to as the **mid irons** and the 8, 9, and pitching wedge are referred to as the **short irons**. The number 1-wood is usually referred to as a driver and may be made of

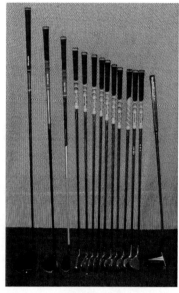

Figure 2.3

Differences in lengths

Figure 2.4a

Figure 2.4b

Figure 2.4c

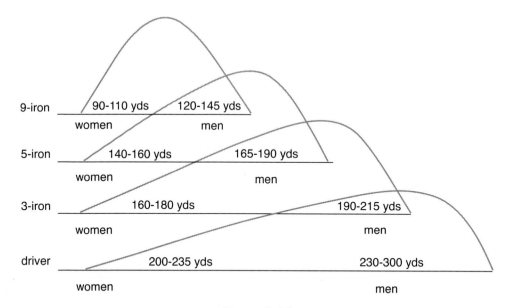

Figure 2.4d

Range of approximate distances for average golfers

wood or metal. The number 2, 3, 4, and 5 woods are referred to as fairway woods. These woods acquire their name because they are normally hit from the fairway.

There are two basic club head designs. One is referred to as a **blade** and the other is a **cavity back**. In the picture below the club head on the left is an example of a blade and the one on the right an example of a cavity back (see figure 2.5). Cavity back clubs are usually termed as game improvement clubs. The weight has been taken out of the middle of the club and redistributed around the perimeter. This makes the club more forgiving on off-center hits and makes it easier to get the ball up in the air with the long irons.

The two basic materials that shafts are most often made of are **graphite** and **steel**. In the picture on the next page, the shaft on the left is made of graphite and the one on the right is made of steel (see figure 2.6). The benefits of graphite as opposed to steel are that the overall weight of the club can be lightened thus allowing an increase in club head speed. The drawbacks of graphite are that it is difficult to control the consistency of the **flex point** (where the shaft bends) and the **torque** (the amount that the club head turns when it contacts a ball). Graphite shafts can be much more expensive than steel. The cost of a graphite shaft increases as the shaft's playing characteristics come closer and closer to resembling those of a steel shaft. In other words,

Figure 2.5

the more you can make a graphite shaft perform like a steel shaft the more expensive it will be. The faster the club head speed the stiffer the shaft must be in order to maintain control. Shafts come in a variety of flexes. The letters X, S, R, and L with X representing an extra stiff shaft, S representing a stiff shaft, R representing a regular shaft, and L representing a very whippy shaft, usually designates the flexibility or stiffness of the shaft. The faster the club head speed the stiffer the shaft must be.

There are two types of bags used to carry your clubs. There are bags made for riding in a cart and bags made for those who wish to walk. The picture below is that of a cart bag. Cart bags are much larger than walking bags and have plenty of storage space. Touring professionals use these bags because of the large amount of storage they provide. Walking bags like the one pictured below are much lighter than cart bags. Other accessories include a glove for ensuring a firm grip on the club, tees for raising the ball off the ground (on the tee box only), shoes to help eliminate slipping, hats to protect you from extended exposure to the sun, and of course balls. Golf balls today are much different from those of the past. They have a variety of covers as well as multiple layers and are designed to travel much farther and stop much quicker on the greens than earlier versions.

Graphite Steel

Figure 2.6

Caps

Tees

Lightweight carry bag

Golf ball

Cart or tour bag

Golf shoes

It is not recommended that beginners purchase new and expensive equipment. The importance of purchasing equipment that fits you will be discussed in the next chapter. In the beginning it is strongly suggested that you either borrow equipment or purchase equipment that is relatively inexpensive.

Scoring

The number of strokes that it takes you to finish the hole including any misses and/or penalties determines your score on each hole. Your score for the round is simply the total of your strokes for the 18 holes. There are two types of play, **Stroke play** and **Match play**. In stroke play you simply play and the person with the fewest number of strokes at the end of the round wins. In match play you play by the hole and the person winning the most holes wins the match.

Each hole is assigned a numerical value called **par.** Each golf course consists of holes that have par values of 3, 4, and 5. Par for a hole is determined by factors such as length and difficulty. Par on any hole is simply a standard of excellence we all go by. Par 3 holes range in length from 50-265 yards. On a par 3 hole allowing you one tee shot and two putts theoretically determines the par standard of excellence. Holes ranging from 275-490 yards in length are usually referred to as Par 4s. On a par 4 hole allowing you one tee shot, an approach to the green shot, and two putts determines the par standard of excellence. The longer holes ranging from 500 to 600+ yards are called Par 5s. On par 5 holes allowing you a tee shot, two approach shots, and two putts determines the standard of excellence for par.

Sometimes we make a score that is higher or lower than the par value on a hole. One stroke higher than par on any hole is called a **bogey.** Two strokes over par is a **double bogey,** and three strokes over par is a **triple bogey.** One stroke better than par is called a **birdie.** Two strokes better than par is an **eagle** and three strokes better than par is a **double eagle.** If your scores total higher than the par value you are said to be over par and if your scores total lower than the par value you are said to be under par. Par on most courses is 72 and consists of 18 holes. On most courses, there are normally four par-3 holes, four par-5 holes, and ten par-4 holes.

On the next page is an example of a scorecard. (See figure 2.7) The card provides you with valuable information such as the distance of each hole from the different tee markers, the par value for each hole, the handicap rating for each hole, and the course rating. The card may provide information about local rules, distances from tee markers in the fairway, and out of bounds. It also provides you with spaces to keep your score hole by hole.

The Handicap System

Golf has an extremely unique handicap system that allows players of different skill levels to compete against each other on the same playing field. The system takes in considera-

TEES PLAYED BLUE □ WHITE □ RED □	DATE:	SCORER:								ATTEST:										RATING	SLOPE		
BLUE	348	360	165	566	350	414	603	192	345	3343	332	360	510	200	385	176	417	540	361	3297	6640	71.4	122
WHITE	340	320	120	526	335	354	590	140	325	3050	325	315	470	192	365	163	392	493	341	3075	6125	68.7	116
MEN'S HDCP.	12	8	16	4	10	6	2	18	14		13	11	5	15	1	17	7	3	9				
MEN'S PAR	4	4	3	5	4	4	5	3	4	36	4	4	5	3	4	3	4	5	4	36	72		
HOLE NO.	1	2	3	4	5	6	7	8	9	Out	10	11	12	13	14	15	16	17	18	In	Tot	HDCP	Net
MEMBER NO.																							
LADIES' PAR	4	4	3	5	4	4	5	3	4	36	4	4	5	3	4	3	4	5	4	36	72		
LADIES' HDCP.	14	12	18	4	10	6	2	16	8		11	13	5	15	1	17	7	3	9				
RED	305	295	105	496	315	334	495	105	305	2755	298	285	430	170	340	146	362	458	321	2826	5581	70.2	114

Figure 2.7

tion the difficulty of the course you play and the scores that you shoot. A handicap is then given to you according to the information gathered. Handicaps are figured in the following way. Take the scores from your last twenty 18-hole rounds and throw out the 10 worst scores then average the remaining 10 scores to come up with an average score. Your handicap will be determined by taking 96% of the difference of your average score minus the course rating. For example, if your average is 88 and the course rating on the course you play is 71.5 it can be said that you average about 16.5 strokes above the course rating per round. If you take that number (16.5) and multiply it by 96% then round it to the nearest whole number the answer will be your handicap. Therefore, your handicap would be15. (See figure 2.8)

When you play against others, your handicap will determine the number of strokes you must give or the number of strokes you will receive. Since each course has its own course rating your handicap will be adjusted for the difficulty of the course you play. For example, a player with a 10 handicap at a course that has a rating of 75.6 would be a more skilled player than one with a 10 handicap at a course that has a rating of 69. The **course rating** tells us the difficulty of the course. The higher the course rating the harder the course will play. The length and the degree of difficulty of the holes determine the course rating

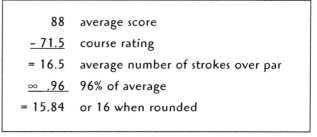

Figure 2.8

Determining your handicap

```
   88    gross score

 - 15    handicap

 = 73    net score
```

Figure 2.9

Determining your net score

at each course. Factors such as hazards, fairway size, thickness of the rough, and severity of the greens are all used to help establish a course rating. Holes on each course are rated with the easiest being the 18th handicap hole and the hardest being the number 1 handicap hole.

When you play a tournament, you will be given a stroke on each of the handicap holes that represent your handicap. If you have a three handicap then you will receive a stroke on the number 1, 2, and 3 handicapped holes on the course. If you are playing against someone with a nine handicap they will be given a stroke on each of the 9 most difficult holes. The winner will be the player with the lowest **net score.** To find your net score you take your **gross score** (the score you actually shot) and subtract your handicap. The result is your net score and is the score used to determine the winner. (See figure 2.9) This handicapping system is part of what makes golf such a great game and one that can truly be enjoyed by everyone who wishes to play.

Name _____   Section _____

Chapter Two Review

1. What do you call the area in which play must begin on each hole?

   _____

2. Define the area on the course known as rough.

   _____

   _____

3. List three different positions in which the clubface could be when it makes contact with the ball. _____ _____ _____

4. How many clubs are you allowed to carry during a round of golf?

   _____

5. Which club will hit the ball farther, a 2-iron or a 7-iron?

   _____

6. Which club has more loft, a 6-iron or a 9-iron?

   _____

7. What two basic materials are shafts constructed from? _____

   _____

8. What is the difference between stroke play and match play?

   _____

   _____

9. One over par is referred to as a _____ and one under par is referred to as a _____.

10. List three bits of information you can get from a scorecard. _____

    _____

11. If your average score is 78 and the course rating where you play is 67.8 what would your handicap be? _____

12. What is the difference between your gross score and your net score?

    _____

13. What is your favorite brand of equipment and why? _____

    _____

    _____

    _____

CHAPTER THREE

THE IMPORTANCE OF EQUIPMENT

Differences in Equipment

Understanding equipment today almost requires a college degree. The materials used to build the equipment alone certainly require an extensive study of the periodic table. Terms like titanium, urethane inserts, inverted cones, tuned weight cartridges, trampoline affect, coefficient of restitution, moment of inertia, center of gravity, and the list goes on are enough to confuse a Rhodes Scholar. Every year this technology produces clubs that promise 20 more yards off the tee. In 1992, John Daly led the tour in driving distance-averaging 283.4 yards per drive. If you add 20 yards per year due to improved equipment this year's average driving distance for John should have been 483.4 yards. In 2002 John Daly lead the tour in driving distance again with an average drive of 309 yards, which is a bit short of that 483 mark.

The truth is one cannot purchase a golf game. The best equipment in the world will not cure a reverse pivot, an early release, or that dreaded chicken wing that has plagued my good friend Dr. Couey for so many years. **Although purchasing good equipment will not by itself help your game, purchasing good equipment that fits you will.**

Most people, upon taking up the game of golf, immediately purchase new equipment. The equipment they buy usually resembles that of which their favorite player plays. It is not uncommon to see a junior who has just taken up the game carrying a 45-inch extra stiff 7-degree Nike driver simply because Tiger Woods plays that club. It is usually not a good idea to have a club in your bag that's taller than you. Using a club designed for Mr. Tiger Woods is however a good way to be acquainted with "Mr. Alwaysinthe Woods". It is extremely important that your equipment fits you and your swing. As a beginner you haven't developed fundamentals much less a golf swing and should put purchasing expensive equipment off until you have taken a few lessons and have developed some solid fundamentals.

When you are ready to purchase equipment consult with your local PGA professional, and he or she will be able to guide you in the proper direction. There are many different brands of clubs, balls, putters, and woods available today. Companies like Nike, Titleist, Wilson, Cleveland, Taylor Made, Callaway, and Hogan are just a few of the manufacturers that make golf equipment. All pro line equipment purchased today is going to be quality equipment. Most manufacturers offer two types of irons, **traditional** and game **improvement**. Traditional clubs are usually preferred by the pros, because they like to work the ball (make it change directions in the air). Game improvement clubs are much more forgiving and are hands down the better choice for 98% of all others who play the game.

The Importance of Club Fitting

In this section we will discuss the importance of club fitting, the process of fitting, and what can be accomplished by having a set of clubs custom fit to you. Hopefully, after finishing this chapter you will have a better understanding of the playing characteristics of equipment and how it affects your golf swing.

Your swing is as unique as your fingerprint. Most golfers continually adjust or make swing changes to compensate for poorly fitted equipment. In order to maximize your game, your clubs need to be custom fit to your personal swing and club preference.

> *No matter how much you practice or how many lessons you take, if your equipment doesn't fit your swing, you're playing with a handicap.*

Lie Angle and Length

Making sure your clubs have the correct **lie angle** (the angle made between the shaft and the club head) is extremely important if your desire is to hit shots that are directionally consistent. If a golfer has the improper lie angle on his clubs he will more than likely be plagued with directional problems. Clubs with too upright a lie will have a tendency to pull the ball left of the target and will increase the possibility of imparting a hooking spin to the ball. Conversely, clubs with a lie that is too flat will have a tendency to push the ball right of the target, and will increase the possibility of imparting a slicing spin to the ball. (See figure 3.1)

Correct lie   Lie too upright   Lie too flat

Figure 3.1

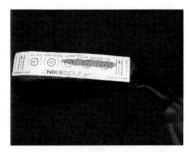

Figure 3.2

Since the shaft of a club flexes throughout the swing and the arms have a tendency to extend through the impact area, the only true way to determine the correct lie angle is by using a hitting board and some tape. By placing tape across the sole of the club and hitting balls off a hitting board, you will be able to determine what part of the sole of the club hits the ground. If the tape has contact marks towards the heel, then the lie angle is too upright; if the marks favor the toe than the lie angle is too flat. (See Figure 3.2)

The **length** of your club is equally important. If the length is incorrect, the result is off center hits (hits away from the center of the club). Off center hits are responsible for a lack of distance control as well as directional problems. A ball hit off the toe, for example, will travel a shorter distance than a ball hit in the center of the club. To determine the correct length and lie angle most professionals use a fitting system like the one shown to the left. (See figure 3.3) The system is equipped with clubs that vary in length and lie. Clubs can be alternated throughout the fitting session until the correct match is determined for the player. Having clubs that are the correct length and have the correct lie will greatly increase your consistency.

The illustrations below (See figure 3.4) show how face tape can be used during a fitting session to determine off center hits.

Figure 3.3

Dyna-fit Fitting system

Figure 3.4

Shaft Flex and Materials

A golf shaft has three important elements. They are:

1. Shaft flex or stiffness
2. Material and weight
3. Flex point or bend

Shaft flex or stiffness is the amount the shaft bends and greatly influences such factors as distance and direction. Choosing the right flex is important in order to get the most out of your swing. Most amateurs play with clubs that are too stiff. The assumption that men need stiffer club shafts, and that ladies' clubshafts must be very flexible, is usually incorrect. Generally speaking the slower the swing speed the more flexible the shaft must be in order to produce maximum distance. Conversely, the faster the swing speed the stiffer the shaft must be to maintain control. Like most everything in life there is always a trade off, gaining control usually means giving up distance. A shaft too stiff tends to cause the ball to have a lower trajectory whereas a shaft too flexible tends to elevate the ball higher.

Another contributing factor is the **"kick point"** or the point where the shaft bends during the swing. If the shaft flex point is too high the resulting trajectory will tend to be too low, and if it's too low the resulting trajectory will be too high. High flex points are generally preferred by better players, and lower flex points are for less skilled players. To determine the right kick point for your clubs requires analysis from a trained professional. Many feel they can decide simply by using swing speed as an indicator. However knowing the swing speed sometimes can be of little value if you don't fully understand the other principles. For example, let's say two individuals have the same swing speed, 100 mph, and it has been determined that they both need a stiff shaft. Let's say they hit a demo club with a low kick point and a stiff shaft. The more skilled player hits the ball with a normal trajectory while the less skilled player hits the ball in a lower trajectory. The question is what could have caused the difference? The difference comes from the player's rate of acceleration through the ball. Just because they have the same swing speed does not mean they accelerate the same through impact. For example, suppose both golfers were in separate sports cars and from a dead stop accelerated to 100 mph with the gas pedal all the way to the floor. As the cars pass 90 mph one keeps the pedal down and accelerates at an accelerating rate until reaching 100 mph. The other driver reaches 90 and then backs off the gas pedal slightly, still accelerating but at a decelerating rate. The second golfer is still accelerating but the rate is different. His swing is picking up lesser speed over equal time intervals. Both golfers reach 100 mph during their swing, however they reach that speed at different times.The true key is where they release their hands. Thus, to correctly determine the proper flex point, both speed and ball trajectory must be taken into consideration.

The weight of a golf shaft and its balance point can definitely affect the flex feel and playing characteristics of a club. The heavier a shaft the stiffer it will play. Again there is a trade off. Heavy shafts play like stiffer shafts; you hit the ball much straighter, but must anticipate a loss of distance. Shafts are made of so many different materials today that it's really hard to keep abreast with the changing knowledge about them. There are basically 2 types of shafts, **graphite** or **steel.** Graphite can be extremely expensive or very cheap. It is lighter than steel and tends to be inconsistent in regards to control. Flexible shafts generally have problems with controlling **torque**(the amount the club face opens or closes when it strikes the ball). The new Fat Shaft design by Wilson is unique in that it has a larger tip diameter. This reduces torque considerably thus allowing one to choose a somewhat more flexible shaft, which in turn produces more club head speed and longer shots, but without the inconsistencies that accompany flexible shafts due to increased torque.

Grip Size, Grip Materials, and Swing Weights

The size of the grip on your club is more than just a little important. An improper grip size can greatly influence a number of factors in the golf swing. The proper grip size should give the golfer a comfortable feeling at address, positive control during the swing, and should not inhibit wrist action as the club head moves into the impact zone.

A grip that is too large can produce the following:

- Decreased feel in the fingers.
- Inhibit wrist action thus affecting the release.
- Cause the player to choke down effectively making the club shorter and resulting in a loss of distance due to a lack of club head speed.

A grip that is too small can produce the following:

- Cause the club head to twist at impact.
- Cause the golfer to squeeze too tightly thus inhibiting proper wrist action
- Cause the golfer to hold the club too close to the butt of the grip, causing a loss of control at the top of the swing.

Once you have developed a swing and are ready to purchase equipment it is strongly recommended that you have your local PGA professional fit you properly. Since different equipment manufacturers have different specifications for their equipment, it is suggested that you have a professional, who carries the brand of equipment you wish to purchase, do the fitting. As far as choosing a specific brand of equipment the choice is ultimately yours. The equipment must look and feel good to you and not someone else.

Periodically you should have your equipment checked. Extended use can sometimes cause the playing characteristics to change. As you work to further develop your swing, it too will change, and may warrant having your club specifications altered. For example, as your swing progresses and becomes more fluid your club head speed will increase, your hands will be in a better position at impact, and the stiffness as well as the flex point of the shaft may need to be altered to achieve the proper ball flight for your new swing.

Perhaps nothing is more important in golf than confidence. Developing and maintaining confidence is something all golfers struggle with. Confidence starts with knowing that your equipment is the best equipment for you and your game. When the time is right " Get Fit".

Chapter Three Review

1. What would be the result of having too upright a lie angle?

   _____

   _____

2. What would be the result of having too flat a lie angle?

   _____

   _____

3. If your clubs are too long where on the clubface will you tend to hit the ball?

   _____

4. What are the three important elements of the golf shaft? _____,

   _____, _____

5. Define shaft flex? _____

   _____

6. Define kick point? _____

   _____

7. What is the resulting trajectory of a shaft that is too stiff? _____

   _____

8. What is the trade off for playing a stiffer shaft versus a more flexible one?

   _____

   _____

9. Decreased feel and inhibited wrist action are evidence of a grip being too large or too small? _____

10 The club head twisting at impact can be caused by a grip that is too large or too small? _____

11. What other club characteristic could cause a club head to twist at impact?

   _____

12. Why should you periodically have your club's playing characteristics checked?

   _____

   _____

   _____

   _____

CHAPTER FOUR

RULES AND ETIQUETTE

General Rules

The Royal and Ancient Club of St. Andrews introduced the first written rules of golf in the mid 18th century. Those first 13 rules are still the nucleus of the rules used to govern the sport today. As the sport grew so did the need for an overall rules authority. This responsibility was assigned solely to the Royal and Ancient Club of St. Andrews until 1952. The United States Golf Association (USGA) and the R&A came together that year to form a unified code. The two organizations meet on a regular basis to constantly improve upon the rules and ensure that the integrity of the game stays intact. The R&A now has well over 125 affiliated countries, associations and unions. It does not impose the Rules of Golf, but governs by consent so that anyone who wants to play the true game of golf plays by the rules.

The rules of golf are as unique as the game itself. Golf is perhaps the only sport in which the player penalizes himself when a rules infraction occurs. Learning and applying the rules is the responsibility of everyone who plays the game.

This chapter serves as an introduction to the rules of golf. Upon completion you should be familiar with some of the basics rules needed to begin playing the game. A more in-depth study of the rules is advised and can be accomplished by purchasing a USGA Rules book and reading it, more than once!

Rules infractions always result in one of three penalties, one-stroke, two-strokes, or disqualification. There is a simple way to remember which penalty applies to each infraction. If the infraction is due to a **lack of ability** by the player, the penalty is **one-stroke.** An example of a "lack of ability" rules infraction would be when a player hits his or her ball into a water hazard. If the infraction is due to a **lack of intelligence** by the player, the penalty is **two-strokes.** An example of a "lack of intelligence" rules infraction would be when a player breaks a rule such as having more than 14 clubs in his or her bag. And if the infraction

cannot be rectified due to stated rules the penalty is **disqualification.** An example of a "cannot be rectified" rules infraction would be when a player signs for a score lower than he or she actually made.

Remember knowing the rules are the responsibility of each player. If you break a rule simply because you did not know it was a rule, it is considered a lack of intelligence and will cost you two-strokes. Below are examples of a few basic rules, all of which carry a two-stroke penalty

- You are only allowed to carry 14 clubs in your bag during a competitive round of golf.
- You may not touch your club to the ground before playing from a hazard or sand trap.
- You may not repair spike marks in the line of your putt.
- You may not putt with the flagstick in the hole when you are on the green. If you do so and the ball strikes the pin it is a two-stroke penalty.
- You may not ask for advice from another player other than in areas of common knowledge such as course information.
- You must always play your ball in the teeing area when you are on a tee box.

Certain rules are applied more frequently than others. When playing a round of golf the rules most frequently encountered are: out-of-bounds, hazards, lost balls, and situations that require a second ball or a provisional ball be played. Whether you are an experienced player or a beginner learning these rules is a must. Spend ample time learning the following rules and how they are applied. Buy a USGA Rules book and mark each one of the following rules with a highlighter. This will make referring to the rules later easier as well as begin to familiarize you with the rulebook and how it is used.

Hazards

There are two types of water hazards on the golf course, **regular** water hazards and **lateral** water hazards. Regular water hazards are hazards that usually lie between the player and the hole and are always defined by **yellow** stakes or lines. Lateral hazards are usually hazards that do not lie directly between the player and the hole and are always defined by **red** lines or stakes. There are several options afforded you when your ball comes to rest in a water hazard. The options vary according to the type of hazard; therefore it is important to determine if the hazard is a regular hazard or a lateral hazard before you take relief. It is possible for the ball to come to rest within the boundaries of the hazard and not be in the water. **If the ball comes to rest inside the stakes or the line defining the hazard, it is considered to be in the hazard even if it is not in the water.** When playing from a hazard you may **not** ground your club; if you do so it is a two shot penalty.

When your ball comes to rest in a regular water hazard you have the following options:

- You may play your ball, as it lies, no penalty.
- You may play the ball from the previous spot from which you played and add a penalty stroke.
- You may keep the point at which the ball entered the water between you and the hole and go back as far as you want on that line, then drop and add a penalty stroke.

When your ball comes to rest in a lateral water hazard you have the above options plus the following options:

- You may drop the ball within **2 club-lengths,** no nearer the hole, at a spot where your ball last crossed the hazard with a penalty of one stroke.
- You may go to the other side of the hazard, equal distance from the hole, drop and add a penalty of 1 shot.

Lateral hazards give you the extra two options because it is not always possible to get to the other side, thus eliminating your ability to keep where the ball entered the hazard between you and the hole. On all the above options you must count the stroke that put you in the hazard.

The best way to play from a water hazard is to stay out of them.

Out of Bounds

Out-of-bounds is an area on the golf course from which play is prohibited. Out-of-bounds is usually defined by white stakes or a white line painted on the ground but can be defined by fences or roads. **For a ball to be out of bounds the entire ball must be out-of-bounds.** When a white line painted on the ground marks the boundary, the ball is said to be in bounds if any part of the ball touches the line. When stakes are used to define the boundary, an imaginary line, extended from the front edge of one stake to the front edge of the next stake, is the line used to determine if the ball is in or out-of-bounds. If any part of the ball touches the line the ball is in bounds.

The penalty for hitting a ball out-of-bounds is **stroke and distance**. This means you must return to the previous spot from which you played, play again and add a penalty shot. Remember to count all the strokes including the one that caused the ball to go out-of-bounds. If the ball was on a tee you may re-tee it; if not you must drop it as close as you can to the previous spot.

There are three basic reasons for out-of-bounds to be present on a golf course:

- It keeps golfers off of private property surrounding the course.

  Selling real estate on the course is quite lucrative. This causes course designers to lay out the course in such a way as to have the maximum number of lots available for sale, thus more private property surrounding the course. Most property owners frown on shots being played from their flowerbeds.

- It protects golfers on certain parts of the course from being hit by golf balls.

  The shortest distance between two points is a straight line. Holes are sometimes laid out in a way that encourages one to shorten the distance by hitting his ball in a path that endangers others. Out-of-bounds is used to discourage that type of aggressive play.

- It encourages golfers to play certain holes the way the holes were designed to be played.

  Sometimes courses are laid out in confined areas. For the hole to have adequate length it is necessary to bend it in such a way that makes it vulnerable. To compensate, the risk versus reward factor is only present with the presence of out-of-bounds.

Lost Balls

A ball is said to be lost if the ball cannot be found within 5 minutes of when the search begins, or if the player abandons the ball. A lost ball is played the same as a ball that is out of bounds; you must return to the previous spot and play another ball as well as add a penalty shot. A player may deem a ball to be lost and play accordingly; however if the original ball is found by anyone before the player plays his next shot, then the ball is not lost and must be played by the player.

Provisional Balls/Second Balls

Many golfers are simply unsure of exactly what a provisional or a second ball actually is, much less the proper use of each. For this reason most golfers fear putting another ball in play—and rightfully so since failure to do so properly could result in disqualification. Is it important that golfers know how to play a provisional or second ball? The answer to the above question for anyone who has played golf on a regular basis and has found themselves in one of the following situations is easy: a) standing on a tee box watching a member of the six-some in front of you walking back up a fairway to re-hit his or her tee shot or actually having to make that dreaded walk yourself, or b) finding your ball in a situation in which you feel you are entitled a drop; however, you can get no one in your group to agree, and for a lack of understanding of how to proceed, you simply play on.

If you have found yourself in one of the above situations, you can better understand the need for provisional and second balls. For those who compete regularly, understanding the two are a must. A provisional ball can save time and ease the speed of play problems that arise in competition. A second ball gives everyone who is unsure or uneasy about how to proceed a simple option. Learn what provisional and second balls are, how they differ, and when and how to use each. This will take away the fear and help you become a more complete golfer.

Rule 27-2: A provisional ball may be played when the original ball is thought to be *out of bounds* or is *lost outside a water hazard*.
To play a provisional ball, you should:

- Verbally state the intent to play a provisional ball prior to doing so. If the intent is not stated and another ball is played, the second ball played is not eligible to be a provisional ball and becomes the ball in play under penalty of stroke and distance.

- Mark the provisional ball in such a way that all members of your group may easily distinguish it from the original ball.

- Play the provisional ball up to, but not beyond the point where the original ball is thought to be. (If a stroke is played past this point, the original ball is deemed lost and the provisional ball becomes the ball in play under penalty of stroke and distance). If the original ball is found and is "in play", then the provisional ball shall be lifted. If the original ball is not found or is " out of play" the provisional ball becomes the ball in play.

Rule 3-3: A second ball is a ball that is played *along with the original ball* when one is unsure of his or her rights as to how to proceed.
To play a second ball, you should:

- Verbally state the intent to play a second ball prior to doing so. If the intent is not stated and another ball is played, the second ball played becomes the ball in play under penalty of stroke and distance.

- Mark the second ball in such a way that all members of your group may easily distinguish it from the original ball.

- Play the original ball as it lies. Put the second ball in play from the position you feel as though you should have been allowed to play from.

- Finish the hole with both balls, and record both scores.

- Mark the spot where the original ball lay so it may be easily found and the situation recreated for the rules committee.

- Inform the rules committee of the situation before you sign your card.

Never put another ball in play simply for the sake of doing so. Provisional and second balls should be used with respect and only when called for. This is not to say one should fear using them. Simply learn them, learn how and when to use them, and then do so with respect. If you have further questions regarding provisional or second balls, consult your local PGA professional.

Taking a Drop

From time to time you will find yourself in a situation in which you may have to take relief. For example, let's say your ball has come to rest on a cart path. You are entitled free relief and may pick up your ball and drop it within 1-clublength of the path no nearer the hole without penalty. Let's say your ball comes to rest in a lateral water hazard. You may take relief within 2 club-lengths of where the ball entered the hazard no nearer to the hole and there is a penalty of 1 stroke. When taking relief you are entitled to either a one or two club-length drop. A good way to remember how many club-lengths you are entitled to is by remembering the following; If a **penalty stroke** is involved you receive **two club-lengths;** if **no penalty** is involved you only receive **one club-length**

Pace of Play

Although golf is one of the world's most popular sports it's not without its problems. **The most prevalent problem in golf is pace of play.** An 18-hole round of golf should take between 3 1/2 to 4 1/2 hours to play, depending on if you walk or ride. Unfortunately, weekend rounds can take up to 5 1/2 hours or longer. Rushing around the course is certainly not the answer; after all taking time to enjoy your surroundings, breathing the fresh air, and thinking your way around the course is what golf is all about. The excuse is often made that inexperienced players are the main culprits and while being inexperienced does not help matters, it is but one of the problems that affect pace of play. Below are some things you can do to help keep the pace of play up and the game more enjoyable to all that play.

- Be at the course at least 30 minutes before your tee time. This will give you ample time to get organized, warm up, and be on the first tee when it's your time to play.
- Play from the appropriate tees, tees that match your skill level.
- Never spend more than five minutes looking for a lost ball. After five minutes you must apply the lost ball rule and proceed.
- Never go into water hazards to retrieve balls; once they enter the hazard they are officially property of the golf gods who dwell there. Proceed by applying the rules associated with the type hazard you're in.
- Learn how to play provisional and second balls.
- Unless in a tournament play **"ready golf"**, golf in which the honor system is dropped and who ever is ready plays next.
- When approaching the green, leave your equipment on the side of the green nearest the next teeing area.
- If you are a beginner try to play during non-peak hours.
- Always wave faster players through and in doing so move completely out of the way.

Taking Care of the Course

Taking care of the course is as important as taking care of you. You're at your best when you feel well and others enjoy you more when you're in that state. A golf course is no different. When the course is in good shape everyone enjoys playing it as well as being challenged by it. Taking care of the course is the responsibility of every golfer who plays that day.

Etiquette

Etiquette is best defined as the way in which we treat our playing partners, the golf course, and the way we conduct ourselves while playing the game of golf. Below are some examples of good etiquette in terms of not only taking care of the course but your playing partners and your personal conduct while playing the game as well.

The Golf Course

1. *Always check in with the pro shop before playing.*
2. Always repair ball marks and divots.
3. Always rake sand traps after you have played from them.
4. Never drag your feet on the green.
5. Never leave trash on the course.
6. Avoid excess traffic around the hole.
7. Always replace the flag after finishing the hole.
8. Never take excessive divots while taking practice swings.
9. Never abuse equipment, yours or that of the golf course.

Playing Partners

1. Always treat your playing partners as you would have them treat you; they are not your opponent; the golf course is.
2. Avoid stepping in the putting line of others.
3. Be quiet when others are playing their shot.
4. Be fair in making rulings for yourself and for others.
5. Be sociable; golf is a gentleman's, as well as a woman's game.

Conduct

1. Always dress appropriately; most courses will not allow tank tops or cut offs.
2. Always control your temper.

3. Always play by the rules of golf. If you are involved in a rules infraction be the first to penalize yourself.

4. Keep a good pace; if you're holding someone behind you up let him or her play through.

5. Always be courteous to others you meet on the course regardless of how they treat you.

6. **Set an example for others to follow.**

Safety

Anytime lots of people are together in one place, all carrying a bag full of clubs and trying to hit small round projectiles (that are quite expensive) as far and as straight as they can (in what some might label a feeble attempt in determining the alpha male), only to see those projectiles come to rest in a watery grave some 90 degrees off line, is to say the least somewhat dangerous. Throw in a bad day at work and a not so good haircut and one could find themselves in a "buried lie". Safety is important and should not be taken lightly. It is each player's responsibility to practice safety on the course. Below are a few safety tips you should follow:

• If you hit your ball in an errant direction, always shout **FORE,** the universal word for watch out.

• If you hear the word **FORE,** always duck and cover your head. Never look to see where the yell came from.

• Always wait until the group in front of you is well out of range before you proceed.

• Never throw a club while on the course.

• Stay well behind the person who is next to play.

• Never walk onto a tee box until the previous player has stepped off.

• Before you take a practice swing always look around to make sure everyone else is a safe distance away.

• When holding a club in groups of people always hold it by the club head.

• Never walk into another fairway without looking to see if anyone is playing that hole.

Articles and Laws in Playing at Golf

1. You must Tee your Ball within a Club's length of the Hole.

2. Your Tee must be upon the Ground.

3. You are not to change the Ball which you Strike off the Tee.

4. You are not to remove Stones, Bones or any Break Club, for the sake of playing your Ball, Except upon the fair Green within a Club's length of your Ball.

5. If your Ball comes among watter, or any wattery filth, you are at liberty to take out your Ball & bringing it behind the hazard and Teeing it, you may play it with any Club and allow your Adversary a Stroke for so getting out your Ball.

6. If your Balls be found any where touching one another, You are to lift the first Ball, till you play the last.

7. At Holling, you are to play your Ball honestly for the Hole, and not to play upon your Adversary's Ball, not lying in your way to the Hole.

8. If you should lose your Ball, by it's being taken up, or any other way, you are to go back to the Spot, where you struck last, & drop another Ball, And allow your adversary a Stroke for the misfortune.

9. No man at Holling his Ball, is to be allowed, to mark his way to the Hole with his Club, or anything else.

10. If a Ball be stopp'd by any Person, Horse, Dog or anything else, The Ball so stop'd must be play'd where it lyes.

11. If you draw your Club in Order to Strike, & proceed so far in the Stroke as to be bringing down your Club; If then, your Club shall break, in any way, it is to be Accounted a Stroke.

12. He whose Ball lyes farthest from the Hole is obliged to play first.

13. Neither Trench, Ditch or Dyke, made for the preservation of the Links, nor the Scholar's Holes, or the Soldier's Lines, Shall be accounted a Hazard; But the Ball is to be taken out teed and play'd with any Iron Club.

John Rattray, Capt

Amendment to the Articles & Laws—1758

The 5th, and 13th Articles of the foregoing Laws having occasioned frequent Disputes It is found Convenient That in all time Coming, the Law Shall be, That in no Case Whatever a Ball Shall be Lifted without losing a Stroke Except it is in the Scholars holes When it may be taken out teed and played with any Iron Club without losing a Stroke—And in all other Cases the Ball must be Played where it lyes Except it is at least half Covered with Water or filth When it may, if the Player Chuses be taken out Teed and Played with any Club upon Loosing a Stroke.

Thomas Boswall, Capt

Name _____   Section _____

Chapter Four Review

1. How many clubs are you allowed to carry in your bag? _____

2. What is the penalty for grounding our club in a hazard? _____

3. What color lines or stakes identifies regular water hazards? _____

4. What color lines or stakes identifies lateral water hazards? _____

5. What option is available to the player when in a lateral hazard that is not available to the player in a regular hazard? _____

   _____

6. What color lines or stakes are used to identify out-of-bounds? _____

7. What is the penalty for hitting a ball out-of-bounds? _____

   _____

8. When you are unsure if your ball has come to rest in bounds or out-of-bounds you should play what type of ball? _____

9. What is the difference between a second ball and a provisional ball?

   _____

10. List 3 examples of good etiquette: _____

    _____

11. How do you know when taking relief if it is a one or two club-length drop?

    _____

    _____

12. What should you do if you hit a shot that is headed in the direction of others?

    _____

    _____

CHAPTER FIVE

THE GOLF SWING

The Golf Swing

Hitting a golf ball correctly is about as easy as making a 3 foot putt on a perfectly flat putting surface—well it might not be that hard but it's not easy. The golf swing is relatively simple in theory. Swing the club through the ball, keeping the path the club is traveling as it enters the impact area square to the target while keeping the face of the club square to the target as well. Oh yeah, you must also keep the distance between you and the ground the same throughout the swing and at the same time try to generate some club head speed in order to hit the ball a decent distance while maintaining your balance of course. Let's don't forget about the fact that people are watching you, your mind is trying to organize the 435 swing thoughts you're sending it from all the golf tips you've ever read, and the fact that you know you're about to take the $500 driver that you bought because it's guaranteed to hit the ball straight and long and hit a $5 golf ball into a place where you'll never find it in spite of the mad search that will turn up only poison ivy and a hidden chigger farm—nothing to it.

The truth, is once you develop good fundamentals and learn to put the swing in motion properly, a chain reaction of events can occur and the rest of the swing pretty much takes care of itself—that is if you let it. We will discuss the "if you let it" in more detail in a later chapter. Sometimes learning something as complicated as a golf swing is made far easier if it is learned in stages. In this chapter we will discuss the fundamentals of the golf swing as well as the role played by the arms, hands, legs, torso, and the club. Once you understand the job of each of these components, putting it all together is much simpler than you think.

Take the time to truly learn the fundamentals described in this chapter. Once you have developed a swing that has good fundamentals you will enjoy countless hours of actually playing the game with a minimal amount of practice required. If you place little emphasis on these fundamentals and only partially learn them then more than likely you'll spend more time taking lessons and working on the game as opposed to actually playing it. I've always believed that anything worth doing is worth doing right. As I said earlier in the book, golf is a journey, not a destination. Being a student of the game has been a lifetime occupation for me. In each and every lesson I give I learn something. Practicing and learning the right way are not always easy but it's part of the journey. Challenge yourself and enjoy stepping up to that challenge; be a student of the game and enjoy every stage for each stage has a purpose.

Fundamentals of the Golf Swing

Although there are a number of ways to swing a golf club, some are simply more effective than others. The more complex the golf swing the more difficult it is to repeat. Its been said that golf is not a game of great shots but one of good misses. By keeping the mechanics of the golf swing simple it will be easier to develop a swing that is repetitive. The more repetitive the golf swing the more consistent the misses will be. In order to develop a repetitive golf swing one must first develop good fundamentals. My experience as a PGA teaching professional, working with several thousand students per year, has been that regardless of the skill level every swing fault can be linked to a poor fundamental. A good deal of time should be spent mastering the fundamentals outlined in this chapter.

Fundamentals can be broken down into two areas: **pre-swing fundamentals** (fundamentals used in preparing to make a golf swing) and **swing fundamentals** (fundamentals used during the actual swing itself). Of the two, pre-swing fundamentals are of greater importance than swing fundamentals, especially for beginners. A good setup allows one to make swing errors and still hit a good golf shot while a poor setup requires one to make swing errors to hit a good shot.

Pre-Swing Fundamentals

GPS or grip, posture, and stance are the 3 important pre-swing fundamentals that one must master before moving on to the actual swing. Like a GPS system grip, posture and stance guide us in the direction we must go in order to develop a sound golf swing. The grip is the only contact we have with the club and therefore should be taken seriously. A good grip doesn't necessarily produce a good golf swing, however a bad grip almost always leads to a bad swing. The proper grip allows the club to remain square throughout the swing, thus reducing the role of the hands in squaring the club at impact. Contrary to what you may have read **it is not the rolling of the hands but the rotation of the body that** squares the club at impact. Do not confuse the near absence of hand action with that of wrist action. Wrist action is important in transferring power from the swing to the ball. The way the hands are placed on the club greatly influences the proper wrist action.

Grip

There are 3 basic grips used in golf today: the **10 fingers or baseball grip,** the **interlocking** grip, and the **overlapping** grip. The baseball grip is used mostly by juniors with small hands and is not recommended when the hands become large enough to use one of the other 2 grips. It is referred to as a 10-finger grip because all 10 fingers are placed on the club. The interlocking grip as well as the overlapping grip promotes the hands to work together as a unit by interlocking the pinkie finger of one hand with the index finger of the other or by overlapping the pinkie finger of one hand with the index finger of the other. Golfers with smaller fingers usually prefer the interlocking grip and those with larger fingers prefer the overlapping grip.

Baseball grip   *Interlocking grip*   *Overlapping grip*

There are three basic grip positions: **strong, weak,** and **neutral.** A strong grip is one that has the V's formed by the thumb and the forefinger on both the right and left hand pointing to the right shoulder. A weak grip has the V's pointing between the chin and the left shoulder, and a neutral grip has the V on the left hand pointing between the chin and the right ear and the V on the right hand pointing to the right shoulder. I highly recommend the neutral grip because it encourages the hands to work together as opposed to fighting each other for control. All the above descriptions are based on right-handed golfers; for left-handers the V's will be the opposite.

Strong grip   *Weak grip*   *Neutral grip*

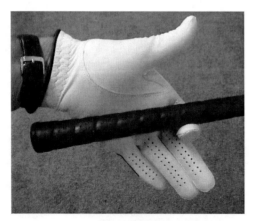

Figure 5.1

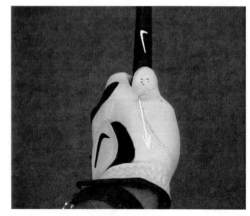

Figure 5.2

Figure 5.3

In taking a neutral grip you should hold the club in such a way that the grip of the club runs diagonally across the hand from under the meaty pad at the base of your palm through your index finger. (See figure 5.1) The index finger creates the sensation of a trigger. When the hand is closed the thumb will be just right of center and the V formed by the thumb and the forefinger should point between your chin and your right ear. (See figure 5.2)

Once your left hand is positioned correctly your right hand can be placed on the club. The right hand holds the club primarily in the fingers where a ring would be worn. (See figure 5.3) The lifeline of the right hand should lie directly on the thumb of the left hand. The V formed by the thumb and the forefinger should point to the right shoulder (see figure 5.4) and there should be a slight gap between the first and second fingers of the right hand.

Grip pressure should be felt in the last three fingers of the left hand, the two middle fingers of the right hand and in the lifeline of the right hand on top of the left thumb. When the hands are positioned on the club correctly you should apply enough pressure to keep the grip firm. A good rule of thumb is to pretend you're holding a bird you do not want to squeeze it to death but you do not want to let it go either.

When the grip is positioned correctly on the club the V formed by the thumb and the forefinger on the left hand will point towards the right ear and the V formed by the thumb

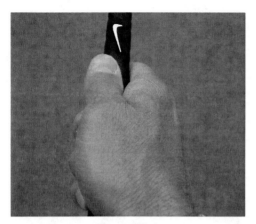

Figure 5.4

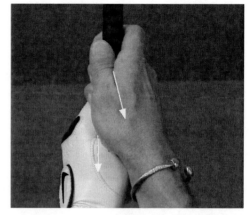

Figure 5.5

and the forefinger on the right hand will point towards the right shoulder. (See figure 5.5). Figure 5.6 illustrates a proper grip when viewed from the front.

Stance

Now that the hands are positioned on the club properly, you must position yourself to the ball correctly. Beginning from the ground up is the best way to approach the setup. The feet should be far enough apart to provide stability yet narrow enough to promote proper leg motion. A good rule of thumb is the shorter the club the narrower the stance, the longer the club the wider the stance. The inside of

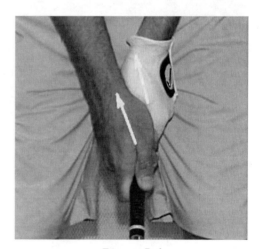

Figure 5.6

the feet should never be wider than shoulder width with the longest club in your bag. Ball position should remain the same (just under the left armpit) with every club in your bag regardless of the width of your stance. What will change slightly is your weight distribution. When using a short club you will have more weight on your left side; as the club gets longer the weight distribution gradually changes until with the longer clubs you have more weight on your right (for right handed golfers). The idea that the ball should be moved in the stance according to what club you're hitting would result in your having a different swing for every club. My experience has been that learning one swing is challenging enough; learning 14 is not healthy. Due to the fact that both arms are the same length and that one hand must be placed below the other when taking your grip, one shoulder will always be lower than the other. If you are right handed then your right shoulder will be lower and the club will hang naturally forward of center in your stance. Playing the ball any farther back than that position will force the shoulders to be shut to your target line. The distance between the left armpit and the ground will be longer and if a proper swing is made, the club would have to travel under ground until it passed a point equidistant in front of the left armpit. For those who wish to argue this point a class in physics would be appropriate. When positioned to the ball properly the head should be behind the ball, slightly with the short irons, and more so with the long irons and woods.

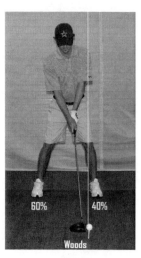

Short Irons   Mid Irons   Woods

Posture

Once you have established the proper ball position and width of stance, the next thing you must do is figure out how far away from the ball to stand, and how much bend or flex there should be in the legs. This is commonly referred to as your posture. **Posture is the single most important fundamental of the golf swing.** Poor posture affects almost every aspect of the swing and is the most frequent cause of swing errors. If the weight is too much towards the heels at the address position (See figure 5.7) the golfer will have a tendency to pick the club during the take away as well as move closer to the ball during the downswing. This results in a multitude of swing errors. If the weight is too much towards the toes at the address position (See figure 5.8) the golfer will have a tendency to take the club to the inside during the take away as well as move away from the ball during the downswing, again resulting in a multitude of errors.

Figure 5.7

Figure 5.8

The proper posture position requires your weight to be evenly distributed between your heels and your toes and your arms to hang naturally down from your shoulders (See figure 5.9). To assume the proper posture position one should start with both feet together even with the ball. Take a small step with your left foot towards the target and a slightly larger step with your right foot away from the target. Flex your knees just enough to insure that you are not standing with your legs locked. Bend from the waist keeping the back straight and the chin up. Allow the arms to hang down until the club touches the ground. Rock

Figure 5.9

your weight back and forth between the heels and the toes until you are on the balls of your feet. With your arms hanging, adjust the distance between you and the ball until the club is centered behind the ball. From time to time check to see if your distance from the ball is correct by taking the right hand off the club and allowing it to hang loosely. If the hand falls towards you then you're too far away; if it falls away from you then you're too close (See figure 5.10)

Too far away from the ball.   Too close to the ball.

Figure 5.10

Alignment

Alignment is the last aspect of the setup that must be discussed before moving on to the swing fundamentals. If poorly aligned to the target it is inevitable that swing faults will soon follow. Achieving proper alignment seems relatively easy yet can require much more attention than first glance might indicate. **If your alignment is incorrect the only way to hit a ball at your desired target is to manipulate both the path of the club and the angle of the clubface at impact.** In simpler terms you must make a bad swing to hit a good shot.

The best way to ensure proper aim is by aligning your body around the position of the clubface. To do this you must make sure you have the clubface aligned at your target. Start by standing behind the ball, looking directly down your target line. Pick a spot on the ground a short distance in front of your ball, which is on the imaginary line between the ball and the target. Place the club head behind the ball so that it is perpendicular to the imaginary line, which runs from your ball through the spot you picked and to your target (See figure 5.11).

Next align your feet, knees, hips, and shoulders parallel to this imaginary line (See figure 5.12).

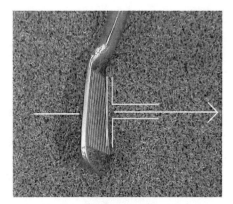

Figure 5.11

Trust that your alignment is correct regardless of what your eyes tell you. Adopt this procedure regularly to ensure this important basic is not overlooked.

The purpose of setting up to the ball properly is to hopefully start a chain reaction of good positions and motions throughout the swing. If you're wrong at the start then the chain reaction will require you to manipulate the club as well as the body in order to get back on track. I cannot stress strongly enough the importance of the setup and the need for you to monitor it on a regular basis. It serves as the foundation for developing a true golf swing. The proper setup will more than likely not feel very good in the beginning. A good rule of thumb is that if it feels good after a couple of days, you're not doing it right. It is highly recommended that you have your local PGA professional help you achieve the proper setup; trying to interpret what you've read, especially as a beginner, is somewhat dangerous since there is a lack of feedback.

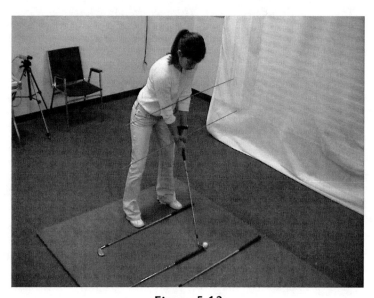

Figure 5.12

Swing Fundamentals

Once you are able to position the body to the ball correctly it's time to move on to the swing fundamentals. The first swing fundamental that must be learned is the **pivot**. Many refer to the pivot as rotation (the turning of your body around your spine). Without a proper pivot, controlling the swinging motion of the club is virtually impossible. A pivot is defined as movement around a fixed point and that's a good description of what is going to happen in the golf swing.

As opposed to one pivot point, however, we will have two, one for the backswing and the movement of weight from the static address position to the right side, and one for the downswing and the movement of weight back into the left side.

The pivot motion provides three important ingredients in the golf swing:

1. a coiling effect where your torso is wound up and loaded like a spring, ready to unwind;

2. a transfer of body weight from one side to the other;

3. consistent tempo or speed.

It is important to learn what your body does in the golf swing before you learn the roles played by your hands, arms, and the club. It has always been easier for me to teach students the proper pivot motion without using a club and especially without using a ball. Learning the proper pivot motion makes it easy to swing the club through the ball as opposed to hitting at the ball with the club. As a fellow instructor once said, "the dog must wag the tail, the tail cannot wag the dog".

The golf swing starts from the address position where the club is basically static. The torso turns around the spine, moving the weight into the right side and then rotates back around the spine, moving weight through the impact area and into the left side in an accelerating fashion. **The rotation of the torso is the power-producing element of the golf swing.** The impression that many have of power stemming from the motion of your hands and arms is a false one. This is not to say that the hands and arms play no role in the golf swing because they do. Power that is generated by the coiling and uncoiling of the torso has to be transferred to the ball through the arms, hands, and the club.

Many believe that you rotate around one pivot point, your head. I personally feel that there are two pivot points, the right hip joint and the left hip joint. Rotating around your right axis point on your back swing and your left axis point on your down swing encourages a turning weight transfer in both directions. It is quite normal, especially during your back swing, for your head to move a little laterally as you turn. A little head movement is desirable; a lot of head movement is not. It is like having a headache; if you take an aspirin it will make you feel better, if you take a bottle of aspirins it will kill you. An incorrect pivot can lead to a number of swing faults, most often what is referred to as a reverse pivot. This occurs when on your back swing your weight does not move around your right axis point but rather hangs on your left side, usually as a result of trying to keep your head still. **For every action there is always an opposite an equal reaction.** As a result, on the down swing the weight moves out of your left side and into your right side, resulting in a multitude of swing errors. The proper pivot motion should have three basic parts. These parts are not separated by a pause, however discussing them individually makes it is easier to grasp the concept:

1. your back swing or your pivot motion into the right side
2. the transition from back swing to down swing as the body changes direction
3. your down swing or pivot motion into the left side more often referred to simply as the down swing

Back Swing

Next to the setup, the backswing is the most important aspect of the golf swing. The start of the back swing sets forth a chain reaction of events. The proper start will set forth the proper chain reaction just as an improper start will set forth an improper chain reaction. The backswing is simply a rotation of the torso around the right axis point. Although there are a number of different opinions as to what part of the body actually initiates the backswing most top instructors believe as I that the torso as a unit starts the swing in motion.

As the torso turns around the spine into the right axis point, the weight moves into the right heel. The head slides slightly to the right and the shoulders turn 90 degrees to the spine angle. The torso continues to turn until the left shoulder is behind the ball and the chest is over the right axis point. Not every part of the body is moving. There must be some resistance with the lower body so as to create a coiling effect between the upper and lower body. This is accomplished by maintaining the angle in the right knee throughout the backswing as well as making sure the weight stays on the inside of the right foot.

As the rotation of the hips and shoulders around the right axis point continues, the resistance between the upper and lower body increases. Do not make an attempt to keep your head still; in fact allow it to swivel to the right to accommodate the rotation of your body. During this rotation feel as though you have a volleyball between your knees. This feeling will help keep the legs solid and allow the left knee to point slightly inward at the top of the backswing while maintaining the proper distance between the knees. When your left shoulder is under your chin, your chest is over your right leg, your back is facing the target, and you feel a stretching sensation in your right thigh due to the resistance between the upper and lower body, you have reached the top of your backswing.

Learning the proper backswing and developing a feel for what actually occurs is much easier to do without using a club. Start by assuming the proper setup position, preferably in front of a mirror. Place your right hand on your left shoulder and your left hand on your right shoulder. Make sure your right shoulder is slightly lower than your left. This is because of how the hands are placed on the club during the actual swing; the right hand is lower than the left hand on the club, therefore the right shoulder is lower than the left shoulder at the address position

Figure 5.13a   **Figure 5.13b**   **Figure 5.14a**   **Figure 5.14b**

(See figure 5.13a-b). While maintaining your spine angle rotate the torso around the right axis point until the left shoulder is behind the ball and the chest is over the right leg. Be sure to maintain the angle in the right knee and keep the weight towards the inside of the foot (See figure 5.14a-b). At the top of your back swing the shoulders should have turned 90 degrees to the target and the hips should have turned approximately 45 degrees.

You should practice making this pivot motion until it feels natural. As demonstrated by the photos below the torso and the legs will look exactly the same when a club is used to make the back swing.

The Transition

Once one has achieved the proper pivot motion and can make a back swing correctly, focus is placed on the next aspect of the golf swing called the transition. At some point the club has to stop traveling back and begin to travel down and towards the ball. This change of direction is called the **transition.** The transition is where the movement of the torso changes directions and the weight begins to shift to the left side. This is a crucial time in the golf swing and must be learned properly. The transition should flow and should have a certain rhythm about it. The most common cause of problems with the transition is a back swing that is rushed thus causing the transition as well as the down swing to be rushed. **One cannot hit a ball with the back swing so the need to generate speed with the back swing is a waste of time.** The more control you have during the back swing the more control you will have through the transition and into the downswing. The purpose of the backswing is not only to put the body and the club in a position to make a good down swing but also **to develop a rhythm for the entire swing.**

Figure 5.15

The legs, more especially the left knee, trigger the transition from backswing to downswing. At the completion of the backswing the left knee moves laterally a few inches while the right knee holds its place. This action stabilizes the lower body, preparing it to accept the unwinding of the torso (See figure 5.15). This transition move sets the tone of the downswing. Ample time should be spent practicing this move until you can feel the difference between a good transition and a not so good one.

Figure 5.16

Downswing

The job your downswing has to do is simple; release all the power that has been built up in the swing thus far. The best way to do this is to have your torso, after moving a little bit laterally, to turn around your left axis point.

If the transition is done properly you will be able to make this move quite easily.

The shoulders for the most part will turn on a fairly level plane. If the right shoulder turns downward too quickly it will be difficult to move properly around your left axis point and your weight will get trapped on your right side. The left leg should firm up considerably as the torso turns around the left axis point (see figure 5.16). With the body rotation almost complete the weight should be predominately on the left side.

Figure 5.17

Your finish position should have you standing fairly erect with a slight spine angle to the right and the right shoulder should be slightly lower than the left. (see figure 5.17).

Next we need to discuss the role of the hands, arms, and the club in the golf swing. In order to hit a golf ball relatively straight the path of the club around the torso and the angle of the clubface at address have to be a certain way. Let's start by discussing the path of the club around the torso. The path the club travels around the torso is called the **swing plane.** The swing plane is determined by the setup. A line drawn up the shaft of the club at the address position represents the proper swing plane (see figure 5.18). As the torso rotates around the right axis point the triangle formed by the arms and the shoulders should remain intact until the hands are about waist high. If the rotation is done properly the club head will remain above the swing plane line (see figure 5.19). At this point the right elbow should begin to fold and the club should start to work above the plane line (see figure 5.20).

As the shoulders and torso continue to rotate, the club will be set above the right shoulder with the left arm, as well as the club face, being parallel to the plane line (see figure 5.21). On the downswing the torso unwinds, the right arm extends, and the

Figure 5.18

Figure 5.19

Figure 5.20

Figure 5.21   **Figure 5.22**   **Figure 5.23**

club will travel back down the plane line into the impact area (see figure 5.22). The arms and the club should stay with the torso until the completion of the swing. At the completion of the swing the right arm should be parallel to the swing plane line (see figure 5.23).

When viewing the swing from above it is clear that the path the club follows is slightly inside on the backswing and slightly inside on the downswing. In other words the club approaches the ball from a bit inside, is square to the target at impact, and travels a bit to the inside on the follow through (see figure 5.24). The club is never forced into a position but is allowed to swing freely throughout the swing. The unwinding of the torso, which swings the arms and thus the club around the spine using centrifugal force, generates club head speed, which is needed to produce distance. If the setup is correct, and the club is allowed to swing freely around the body due to the winding and unwinding of the torso, the club will swing on the proper path through the impact area.

The next area of concern is the role of the hands. The clubface needs to be square to the target line at impact. If the face is not square then a multitude of different shot patterns can occur. The best way to insure that the face is square at impact is to keep the clubface square throughout the swing and the best way to accomplish this is by starting with a good grip.

Figure 5.24

⚹ If the grip is correct the toe of the club will point to the sky when the club is extended parallel to the ground in the backswing (see figure 5.25). At the top of the swing the club-face will be parallel to the left arm (see figure 5.26), and the toe will point to the sky when the club is parallel to the ground in the follow through (see figure 5.27).

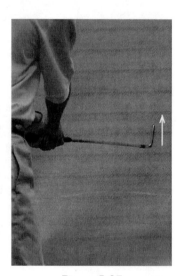

Figure 5.25   **Figure 5.26**   **Figure 5.27**

Balance and rhythm are the last two areas of the swing fundamentals that need to be discussed. It is quite difficult to control the club if you cannot control what's holding the club. An Olympic marksman has no trouble hitting his target while he is standing still but put him on a bull that's bucking and it's a different story. Good balance starts with the legs. The quieter the legs during the golf swing the more balance you will have and the easier it will be to develop a rhythm. Everyone's rhythm is different; some are fast and some are slow. They all have one thing in common; they accelerate the club through the golf ball in a way which allows the club to reach its maximum speed just past the ball.

Basic Ball Flight Laws

In order to be a successful instructor it is necessary to understand the physics behind the flight of a golf ball. To be a successful student you need to at least understand the basic ball flight laws. Feedback is vital to a student's improvement. Understanding some basic principles makes it easier for a student to make minor adjustments during a round as well as provides valuable feedback during practice sessions. **Direction** and **trajectory** are two areas, which can provide students with some insight as to what is occurring in their golf swing. **It is essential that students learn to control the spin as well as the trajectory of the ball.**

Direction

The direction in which a golf ball travels is a result of the spin applied to the ball by the clubface. The spin is a result of two things: the path the club head is traveling and the position of the clubface at impact. The club head can impact the ball from three basic directions: down the line, inside out, and outside in.

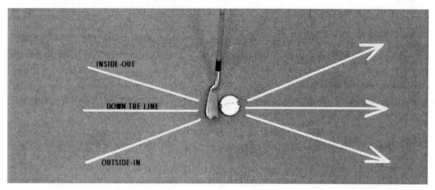

The clubface can be in three different positions when it impacts the golf ball.

Opened   *Square*   *Closed*

The combination of path and face angle can produce an array of different ball flights. Below are a few of the results one should familiarize themselves with.

- A square path with a square clubface results in a straight shot.
- A square path with an open clubface results in a ball that starts right and goes farther right. (Referred to as a pushed fade)
- A square path with a closed clubface results in a ball that starts left and goes farther left. (Referred to as a pulled draw)
- An outside in path with a square clubface results in a ball that starts left then moves to the right. (Referred to as a pull cut)
- An outside in path with an open clubface results in a ball that starts straight and moves rapidly to the right. (Referred to as a slice)
- An outside in path with a closed clubface results in a ball that starts left and continues on that path. (Referred to as a pull)
- An inside out path with a square clubface results in a ball that starts right then moves markedly back to the left. (Referred to as a hook)
- An inside out path with an opened clubface results in a ball that starts right and continues on that path. (Referred to as a push)
- An inside out path with a closed clubface results in a ball that starts straight then moves markedly back to the left. (Referred to as a snap hook)

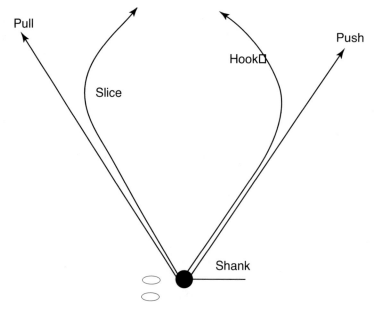

Figure 5.28

Trajectory

Controlling the trajectory of the ball is equally as important as is controlling the spin. There are several ways to control the trajectory of the golf ball.

- You may add or take away loft to achieve certain trajectories by:
    1. Choosing a club that will produce the trajectory you want.
    2. Moving the hands forward or backward in your swing. This will increase or decrease the loft of the club you're holding.
    3. Move the ball backwards or forwards in your swing, this again results in adding or decreasing the loft of the club you are holding.
    4. You may vary the steepness of your swing. A steeper swing will apply much more backspin, which in turn cause the ball to rise more. A swing that is shallow will cause the ball to have less spin, thus resulting in a ball that doesn't climb but bores through the wind.
- You may vary the flex points in your shafts. This is covered in the equipment section of this book.

Though it may appear that choosing the proper club is always the right way to go, it isn't. There are times when the ball must start low and than climb. There are also times when we need to get the ball up quickly but we still need the distance. Lets say your 9-iron is a 135 yard club and you are 145 yards to the hole but behind a tall tree. Your 9-iron will clear the tree but will not make it to the green. You can choose to play a 7-iron, for example, more forward in your stance with the clubface slightly open. This set up will get the ball up as quickly as a 9-iron but due to a longer shaft more club head speed can be generated and the ball will carry farther. Learning to control spin and trajectory will greatly increase one's ability to lower his or her scores.

By learning to control the trajectory of your shots you are providing yourself with many more options when faced with difficult shots. You immediately become a better bad weather player. Learning to control the position of the hands at impact will also greatly improve your ability to trap the ball, which will help you develop into a much better ball striker (See figure 5.29).

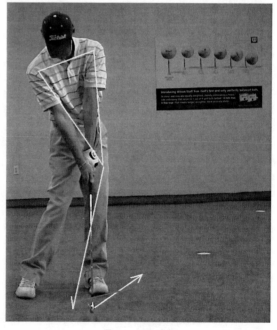

Figure 5.29

Some Do's and Don'ts of the Golf Swing

Do's

- **Do** spend ample time learning the fundamentals. Practice gripping the club and setting up to the ball properly until it becomes second nature.
- **Do** play the ball in one position in your stance until you begin to make consistent and solid contact. Move the ball only when trying to hit a specialty shot and even then only a small increment.
- **Do** allow the head to move slightly to the right during the backswing. Never focus on the head staying totally still but rather on the torso turning around the right axis point.
- When practicing, swing at about 70% of full speed. This will allow you to develop a feel for the different components of the swing as well as when and where these components come into play. It will also help you develop a certain rhythm & tempo in your swing.
- **Do** play at about 80% of your maximum swing speed. Odds are you will be more relaxed, thus reducing tension in the arms as well as the hands, allowing you to generate more club head speed and helping you in actually hitting the ball farther.

Don'ts

- **Don't** practice hitting balls with a poor setup. This only encourages the ingraining of swing faults that will be hard to dismiss later.
- **Don't** raise up or go down during the swing. This causes you to have to make adjustments with the hands, arms, and the legs resulting in a multitude of errors, including the inability to hit the golf ball solidly on a regular basis. Focus on maintaining the angle in your right knee and spine at the address position to help alleviate this problem.
- **Don't** try to keep your head still. This leads to an improper weight shift and makes swinging the club around the body and through the ball on a path conducive to hitting good golf shots extremely difficult. Allow the head to rotate with the torso.
- **Don't** hit the ball as hard as you can on every single shot. This makes maintaining your balance almost impossible as well as destroys any sense of rhythm or tempo you might have.
- **Don't** pick the club up and try to hit at the ball but rather swing the club around the body and through the ball.

- **Don't** try to help the ball into the air; allow the loft of the club to work by swinging down and through the shot.

Drills

- **Leg drill**—identifies the role played by the legs in the golf swing.

  Set up to the ball correctly with a short iron, preferably a 7 or 8 iron. Focus on the flex in the right knee and make a short backswing while maintaining that exact amount of flex (see figure 5.30). Feel as though the hips stay still and only the torso turns. Step out of your right side and into your left during the down swing. Do this by feeling the weight step out of your right foot through the impact area by working of the right instep and by turning the right knee into the left. Finish standing tall on the left leg. Make sure the left foot is flat on the ground and the right foot is perpendicular to the ground with only the tip of the toe making contact with the ground itself (see figure 5.31).

Figure 5.30   **Figure 5.31**

- **Torso drill**—Identifies the role the torso plays in the golf swing.

  Cross your hands across your chest and assume the correct setup position. Focus only on the torso during this drill. Turn the torso to the right around the right axis point. In doing so make sure to maintain the angle in the right knee and force the weight to stay on the inside of the right foot. Allow the torso to continue turning until the left shoulder is behind the ball while maintaining the same spine angle as that of the address position. Allow the lower body to move laterally to the left slightly and then rotate around the left axis point. Make sure the right knee turns in towards the ball and that the shoulders rotate on a fairly level plane. Finish by standing flat on the left foot with the chest facing the target, the left leg firm, and the right knee touching the left. The spine will be tilted slightly to the right and the right shoulder will be slightly lower than the left (see pictures below).

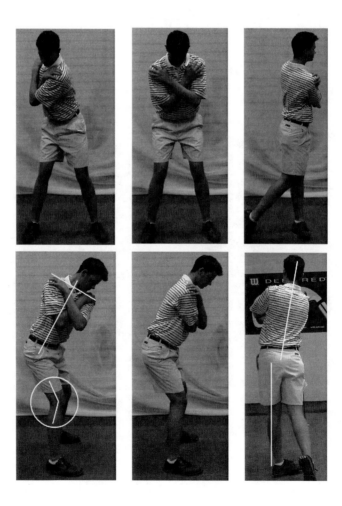

- **The arm drill**—helps develop a feel as to how the arms work around the body. It is especially good in helping develop a feel for the right elbow straightening back out through the impact area. Assume the proper setup position and place your right hand on your left hip. Feel the leg and the torso drills working together as you allow your right arm to swing back and through. Focus on allowing the arm to swing freely around the body (see pictures below).

- **The trap drill**—The purpose of the trap drill is to help the student develop a feel for where the hands are at impact as well as to help them learn to trap the ball. Trapping the ball means that the club strikes the ball before it strikes the ground. This trapping effect imparts good backspin on the ball as well as increases distance due to a better hand position at impact. The best way to do this drill is to use short mini swings with very little wrist action. While keeping the lower body quiet rotate with the upper body around the spine to a position that is about waist high. With the arms fully extended use the torso to turn back down and through the ball into a similar waist high position on the follow through. To begin the downswing allow the lower body to slide slightly forward resulting in more weight being on the left foot at impact. Try to use the big muscles to swing the club back through the ball. In your mind picture your club pushing the ball into the ground and the ball squirting out from underneath the club head (see pictures below).

- **8 o'clock to 4 o'clock drill**—This is a great drill for helping you to develop a feel for how the arms and the torso work together as a unit. Put the butt end of the club in your navel and grip down the shaft until your arms are extended, as they would be at the address position. While keeping the butt of the club connected to your navel, rotate the chest and the triangle formed by the arms and a line across your shoulders to the 8 o'clock position. At this position check to see that the shaft is still perpendicular to your shoulders. Turn thru to the 4 o'clock position and make sure at this position that the club is still in the navel and that the shaft is still perpendicular to your shoulder line. Repeat this drill until you feel the relationship between the arms, hands, and torso in the take-a-way as well as the follow-through. After you have developed the proper feel, try repeating the drill, holding the club correctly.

- **Arm Pull Drill**—This drill will help you feel the right arm straighten through impact as a result of the torso unwinding. This is a much different feel than that of using the right arm to hit the ball. The right arm should remain relaxed and passive throughout the swing. Assume the proper setup position. Grip the club with the right hand only. Take your left hand and grab your right arm just above the elbow. Rotate to the top of the backswing and set the club. To start the downswing, unwind the torso and pull the right arm through using the left arm. Finish in a balanced position facing the target. Swing in a continual motion back and through at about 40% maximum swing speed.

- **Whip Drill**—The purpose of this drill is to help the player develop a feel for setting the wrists and learning to allow the torso to swing the club down and through impact as opposed to the arms. Assume the proper setup position. Allow the club to be taken by the turning of the torso using as little wrists as possible. When the club reaches a position in the backswing where the left arm is parallel to the ground relax your wrists and start pulling the butt end of the club downward almost as if you were trying to crack a whip. When done properly the club will lag behind your hands on the downswing. Remember to relax the wrists at about waist high while the club is still traveling backwards. Make sure to use tempo to do this drill. Too slow will not allow you to feel the whip. This is one time when it's ok to pick up the pace a little.

Name _____   Section _____

Chapter Five Review

1. What does GPS stand for? _____

2. Define pre-swing fundamentals. _____

   _____

3. Define swing fundamentals. _____

   _____

4. List the three most common grips used in golf. _____, _____, _____

5. What is the single most important fundamental in the golf swing? _____

6. With poor alignment the only way to hit a good shot is to do what? _____

   _____

7. What is the power-producing element of the golf swing? _____

8. The change of direction from backswing to downswing is called the _____

   _____

9. The head should remain perfectly still throughout the swing, true or false?

   _____

10. The path the club travels around the body is called? _____

11. You should play at what percent of your maximum swing speed? _____%

12. The direction in which a golf ball travels is a result of _____

    _____

13. What are the path and the clubface position that results in a pull? _____

    _____

14. List two ways to lower the trajectory of a golf shot. _____

    _____

CHAPTER SIX

THE IRON SHOT

The Iron Swing

In discussing the iron shots it is assumed that the fundamentals discussed in the previous chapter are in place. The golf swing is the same for every club; it is the setup that changes slightly. The setup changes due to the different length of each club. It is important to understand how the setup varies with the different clubs. It is also important to spend ample time hitting balls with the different clubs and determining the distance the ball will travel on average with each club. When finding each club's average distance you should hit balls with a swing speed that is about 80% of your maximum swing speed. This allows you to make smooth repetitive swings and will help you determine each club's distance more accurately.

Short Irons

We will define the short irons as the 8-iron thru the sand wedge. Because the irons are shorter you will find yourself closer to the ball. Since you are closer to the ball the swing will be somewhat upright. At the top of the backswing the left arm will be more vertical to the ground (see figure 6.1). The weight at the address position will be slightly forward of center (see figure 6.2) and the backswing will be short of parallel due to the steepness of the swing. As the golf swing gets steeper or more upright the rotation of the torso becomes somewhat limited. Therefore the back swing is shorter than it is with longer irons. Trying to take the club back farther than one is able to rotate will result in a rising up of the body thus changing the distance between the golfer and the ground. On the downswing the golfer will have to return to where he or she began. This up and down motion results in shots being hit fat or thin and in an overall lack of consistency. To hit the short irons properly you must feel as though you are swinging down and through the ball. If done correctly the club will strike the ball before it strikes the ground and the divot made will be slightly past where the ball was setting. Striking the ball before striking the ground is sometimes referred to as trapping the ball. This trapping effect along with the increased loft of the short irons helps to put backspin on the ball causing it to rise quickly and set softly. These irons allow the golfer to land the ball closer to the target and have it stop quickly so as to have a short putt.

Middle Irons

We will define the middle irons as the 5-iron thru the 7-iron. These irons are somewhat longer than the short irons thus requiring you to be a bit farther away from the ball at address. The path the club travels around your body will be somewhat flatter and the left arm will be less vertical than it was with the short irons (see figure 6.1). The weight at the address position will be more centered (see figure 6.2) and the backswing will be just a little short of parallel. The downswing will not be as steep into the ball as that of the short irons due to the flatter position at the top of the swing. You should however still focus on swinging thru the ball with the intent of striking the ball first and then the ground. This will still result in a divot, which originates slightly past where the ball was sitting, as well as one that is much thinner than that made with a short iron. Due to the shallower approach into the ball, as well as the reduced amount of loft, not as much backspin will be imparted on the ball. The ball will therefore roll more when it lands.

Long Irons

The long irons are defined as the 1-iron thru the 4-iron. Because these irons are longer you will be a bit farther away from the ball. This distance from the ball will cause the club to work around the torso on a much flatter plane. Due to the flatter plane the left arm will be less vertical than it was with the middle irons (see figure 6.1). The weight will be more on the right side at the address position (see figure 6.2). Since the club is traveling around the torso in a flatter plane, there will be less restriction thus allowing more rotation and enabling the club to be taken back farther. It is recommended, however, that the club never be allowed to pass a position parallel to the ground. Because the plane is flatter the path thru the ball will be much shallower. This shallower path will result in less spin being imparted on the ball. Less spin results in the ball rolling farther after it hits the ground. Your intent should still be to strike the ball before the club strikes the ground. The divot will be much thinner than that of the middle irons. Focus should be placed on swinging through the ball. Most problems with the long irons result from trying to lift the ball as opposed to allowing the loft of the club to get the ball in the air.

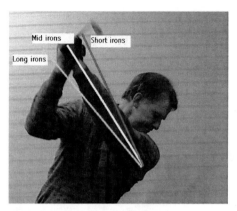

Figure 6.1

Figure 6.2

Some Do's and Don'ts

Do's

- Always hit thru the ball not at it.
- Allow the loft of the club to get the ball into the air.
- Swing at about 80% of maximum when playing.
- Vary the set up with the different irons not the swing.
- Spend time determining how far you hit each iron under normal conditions swinging at 80%.

Don'ts

- Try to over power the ball.
- Help the ball into the air; allow the loft to work for you.
- Swing at the ball but rather thru it.
- Swing at more than 80% of maximum

Drills

- **Mirror drill** —Since it's the setup that changes, not the swing, the best drills are those that focus on the setup itself. Spend time practicing setting up to the ball with different length clubs in front of a mirror. Watch to see how the swing plane changes with each club and try to put a feel with what you see.
- **Rhythm drill**—This drill helps you develop a feel for making consistent swings regardless of the club you're swinging. Without grounding the club swing the club forwards the follow-through position. From this position swing the club back to the top of the backswing and without stopping swing back to the follow through. Keep the club moving between these two positions and begin focusing on feeling a slight increase in speed through the impact area. Take the club back slow and gradually increase the speed through impact and into the follow through. Try to develop a sense of rhythm and feel the rotation of the torso around the spine.
- **Distance drill**—Hit 20-30 balls with each club towards a specific target with a swing that is balanced and in control, usually about 80% of full speed. Step the distance off to the middle of where the balls lay. This distance is approximately how far you will hit each specific club with an average swing. Make a note of each distance and use this information to help you choose the right club for the distance required by the shot. Knowing how far you hit each club is vital in developing a consistent and repetitive golf swing.
- **Board Drill**—Hit balls off of a piece of plywood with an old iron, preferably a 3-iron. This will help you learn to make a shallower swing and use the loft of the club properly.

Chapter Six Review

1. Is a 9-iron considered to be a short, medium, or long iron? _____

2. The plane that a long iron follows around the torso is much _____ than that of a short iron.

3. What % of your maximum swing speed should you use while playing? _____

   _____

4. The divot should be shallower with a long iron than that which is made by a short iron. _____

5. The club should strike the ball before it does the ground with all the irons.

   _____

6. How does backspin affect a golf ball? _____

   _____

7. What is the farthest back any club should be taken in the golf swing?

   _____

8. Problems in hitting the long irons usually result from what?

   _____

9. Taking a short iron to far back usually results in what swing error?

   _____

10. What varies when hitting short, medium, and long irons?

    _____

11. Where should the weight be when hitting middle irons?

    _____

12. It is important to understand what about each club in your bag?

    _____

CHAPTER SEVEN

THE WOOD SHOT

Hitting the woods well is becoming increasingly more important due to the length of the courses built today. The relationship between most golfers and their woods is best described by the opening lines of the Dickens novel A Tale of Two Cities—"It was the best of times, it was the worst of times, it was a time of peace, it was a time of war..." you get the point. Golfers have always had a love hate relationship with the woods. They hit the driver well on one hole and hit it horribly on the next. Hitting the woods well requires a better understanding of the wood swing in general, as well as the proper mental approach to hitting a wood shot.

Because the woods are the longest clubs in the bag, they provide us with the opportunity to hit the ball a long way. Because the woods have the least amount of loft of any of the clubs in the bag they also provide us with the opportunity to hit the ball a long way off line. The length of the clubs allows for increased club head speed, which results in more distance. The decreased loft creates less backspin and more sidespin, which results in more curvature of the ball. It is therefore more important to keep the clubface square thru impact and the club moving on the correct path with the woods than with the other clubs.

The Fairway Woods

Fairway woods are numbered in much the same way as the irons, the smaller the number the longer the club and the less loft it has. The fairway woods can be a tremendous asset when utilized properly. Most of the problems experienced by amateurs arise from trying to hit the ball too far. Like the irons each wood has a specific distance that it should be used for. Trying to hit the wood as far as one can, results in over swinging. This, coupled with the timing requirements of hitting a longer club, usually results in disaster. The fairway woods, when used properly, are actually much easier to hit than the long irons. Due to having more mass

Figure 7.1

in the club head, they have a larger sweet spot (see figure 7.1). The extra mass also makes it easier to get the ball up in the air.

The set-up is similar to that of a long iron. The stance is slightly wider and the weight is more on the right foot. Since the plane is shallow the thought of making a divot should be avoided. More focus should be placed on sweeping the ball off the turf, allowing the loft of the club to get the ball in the air. The speed of the swing should be about 80% of maximum and the intent should be to hit the ball a specific distance. Think more about rhythm and tempo and much less about speed. The better the rhythm and tempo the more relaxed your muscles will be. Without a doubt one can generate more club head speed with relaxed muscles than with tense ones.

The Driver

The driver is simply a longer fairway wood. The biggest difference is that the ball is usually played from a tee. Since the driver has the least amount of loft of all the clubs, with the exception of the putter, it has the largest margin for error. Approaching the driver the same as the fairway woods is the best way to learn control. **Make a balanced and controlled swing at 80% of max, learn the distance the ball will go with that swing, and attempt to hit the ball that distance—no farther.** This approach will help you learn to make smooth golf swings as opposed to unbalanced lunges. The results will be straighter drives, which will lead to more confidence, which will lead to a freer swing, which will ultimately result in more distance. To gain control you must sometimes lose control. Letting the club swing thru the ball as opposed to hitting at the ball is the quickest way to become a good driver.

Although length off the tee is important, it is more important to be able to find your ball—preferably in the fairway. As Harvey Pennick once said "the woods are full of long hitters". Remember confidence is the key to being successful at anything and confidence is very seldom gained by continually failing. Learn to put the driver in play and the distance will come as will the confidence.

Some Do's and Don'ts

Do's

- Always hit thru the ball not at it.
- Allow the loft of the club to get the ball into the air.
- Swing at about 80% of maximum when playing.
- Try to hit the ball a specific distance.
- Spend time determining how far you hit each wood under normal conditions swinging at 80%.

Don'ts

- Try to over power the ball.
- Hit the ball farther than your determined distance with that club.
- Help the ball into the air; allow the loft to work for you.
- Swing at the ball but rather thru it.
- Swing at more than 80% of maximum

Drills

- **Mirror drill**—Since it's the setup that changes, not the swing, the best drills are those that focus on the setup itself. Spend time practicing setting up to the ball with different length clubs in front of a mirror. Watch to see how the swing plane changes with each club and try to put a feel with what you see.
- **Rhythm drill**—This drill helps you develop a feel for making consistent swings regardless of the club you're swinging. Without grounding the club swing the club forwards the follow-through position. From this position swing the club back to the top of the backswing and without stopping swing back to the follow through. Keep the club moving between these two positions and begin focusing on feeling a slight increase in speed through the impact area. Take the club back slow and gradually increase the speed through impact and into the follow through. Try to develop a sense of rhythm and feel the rotation of the torso around the spine.

Chapter Seven Review

1. A fairway wood has more loft than a mid-iron, true or false? _____

2. The driver swing is much steeper than that of a long iron, true or false?

   _____

3. Why is a fairway wood easier to hit than a long iron? _____

   _____

4. The divot should be shallower with a long iron than that which is made by a fairway wood, true or false? _____

5. At what speed should you swing the driver? _____

6. What is the key to becoming a good driver of the ball? _____

   _____

7. What is the farthest back any club should be taken in the golf swing? _____

   _____

8. How does one gain confidence with the driver? _____

   _____

9. What is the most common swing error made when attempting to hit a wood?

   _____

10. Is length off the tee important and why? _____

    _____

CHAPTER EIGHT

THE SHORT GAME

Importance of the Short Game

The first question usually asked by a student taking a lesson is "can you help me lower my scores?". That question can always be answered by the question "do you really want to lower your scores?". All students seem to reply that lowering their score is what they want to do; at any cost they are ready to learn. It is clear most of the time however that what they want to do is learn to hit their driver farther and perhaps improve their long irons a little. When asked to meet me at the short game practice area, many students stand there with driver in hand and look as though they had just lost their best friend.

The driver is always viewed as the problem and for the most part it is. Speaking quite frankly **the driver is the most overused club in the bag.** Golf is a target sport. Hitting your ball to the target in the fewest number of strokes is the key to the game. Most par 4's cannot be reached in one shot, and many par 5's cannot be reached in 2 shots. Since it requires 2 shots to reach a par 4 you may choose to split the distance up any way you like. Take a 350-yard par 4, one could hit a 200-yard tee shot and be left with only a 150-yard approach shot. For most that would mean a 4-iron off the tee and a 7-iron into the green. Hitting a driver as hard as one can in an attempt to hit the ball 300-yards usually results in two mistakes:

1. The ball is hit into a place where the next shot is virtually impossible to put on the green.
2. The ball is hit 300-yards down the middle leaving one with one of the toughest shots in golf and **using the second most overused club in the game, the sand wedge.**

The key to lowering your scores has little to do in the beginning with how far you hit the driver or the ball in general for that matter. **To lower your scores you must make better decisions during the round and you must improve your short game.**

The short game, which is defined as 100-yards and in, is about 70-80% of the game especially for beginners. Developing a good short game is relatively simple to do and is most rewarding in lowering your scores. The mechanics of the short game are much easier than those of the full swing and require less coordination and athletic ability. For the above reason the short game has always been the great equalizer in golf.

Learning the necessary mechanics is easily accomplished in a very short time, feel, however, cannot be taught and must be developed through practice. Therefore it is important to spend ample time working on the short game. A good rule of thumb is that for every hour spent at the range working on the swing spend two at the short game area working on the short game.

Basic Short Game Rules

There are three basic rules that if followed will greatly improve your short game, which in turn will lower your scores.

1. Putt when ever possible. **Putting is the simplest easiest stroke used in golf.** When faced with a shot from just off the green, putting the ball will usually result in the ball starting more on line with the target and rolling closer to the correct distance.

2. When you cannot putt, chip using a club that has just enough loft to carry the ball onto the green. Sometimes extra tall rough or something like a sprinkler head will not allow you to putt the ball. The ball must be carried over this area to land on the green. Choose a club with the least amount of loft as possible to carry the area and land the ball on the green. Many amateurs and some professionals feel that a chip shot requires a wedge or sand wedge. **Getting the ball on the ground rolling towards the hole is the ultimate goal.** A chip shot with a less lofted club will always land and then release towards the hole. A chip shot with a lofted club might spin or checkup thus resulting in a much longer putt.

3. Pitch the ball only as a last resort. **Pitching the ball is a much tougher shot than a chip shot.** You must know how far to carry the ball in the air and how far it will roll once it lands on the green. This requires a tremendous amount of feel as well as a much greater knowledge of the putting surface. Pitch shots leave little room for error and misses are usually much more costly to the golfer's overall score.

Developing a Good Short Game

Developing a good short game requires a proper mindset, the development of good fundamentals, and practice.

1. The proper mindset is important in every aspect of the game. Have a routine and follow it. Decide on the shot you are going to hit and commit to that shot. Expect a positive outcome. Execute the shot as if you are excited to see the outcome not afraid of it.

2. The mechanics necessary for having a good short game are much simpler than those of the full swing. Work hard to learn them properly and spend time perfecting them until they are truly fundamental.

3. Practice is the key to excelling at virtually everything we do. You receive from practice, however, exactly what you put into it. Practice diligently all areas of the short game. Practice putting short putts, lagging longer putts, chipping from different areas around the green with different clubs and from different type lies, and pitching the ball from different distances. **A great way to develop feel is to practice the same shot with many different clubs.**

Consistency is the key to a good short game, and the best way to become consistent is to learn how to hit the shots and then practice hitting them.

Choosing the Right Shot

Choosing the right shot for the situation at hand will yield a better outcome than hitting the wrong shot well. In choosing the right shot there are several factors to consider:

1. The lie of the ball. The lie is always the first thing taken in consideration when deciding on the shot you are going to hit. A good lie may yield several options while a poor lie will yield few. **A good rule of thumb is that the tighter the lie the less lofted the club used (see figure 8.1), the thicker the lie the more lofted the club used (see figure 8.2).**

2. The distance to the hole. The farther from the hole you are the less lofted club you should use. Use enough club to carry the ball onto the green and allow the ball to roll like a putt to the hole.

3. The distance you are from the green. The farther you are from the green the more lofted club you will have to use to carry the ball to the putting surface. A combination of distance from the green and distance from the hole sometimes requires some imagination in choosing the proper club.

Figure 8.1   **Figure 8.2**

4. The intensity of the situation. Where one might try a lofted pitch to really get the ball close to a tight pin when participating in a fun match with friends, a chip shot might be more in order when faced with the same situation to win the US Open. Remember golf is a compromise of what your ego wants you to do, what experience tells you to do, and what your nerves allow you to do. Adding emotion always lessens potential.

Some Do's and Don'ts

Do's

- Putt whenever possible
- Chip using a club with the least amount of loft possible
- Pitch only when you have no other choice.
- Allow the lie to dictate the shot.

Don'ts

- Chip with a lofted club when close to the green.
- Chip with a lofted club from a tight lie.
- Chip with a less lofted club from a thick lie.
- Spend more time practicing your full swing than your short game.

Drills

- **Up and down drill**—This drill is designed to help develop feel as well as an understanding of how each club performs differently. From a spot just off the edge of the green chip one ball to each of the 9 holes on the putting green, then try to make each putt. When you have got up and down to each of the 9 holes, do the same drill, only switch to a different club. Upon completing this drill with several different clubs, move to a spot farther from the green and start over.

- **Three-foot point drill**—This drill is designed to help the student focus when practicing putting short putts. From a distance of about 3 feet putt balls into the hole until you reach a score of 30. You earn a point for every putt you make, deduct 3 points for every putt you miss, and deduct 5 points for every putt you leave short. When you become proficient at this drill back up to a distance of 5 feet and do the same.

- **Must reach the hole drill**—This drill is designed to help develop a feel for rolling the putt just past the hole. This is important since studies show that 98.6 percent of all putts left short do not go in. Start at the first hole on the putting green and putt in order all the way around the green back to where you started. You must one or two putt every hole. If you leave your first putt on any hole short however, you must go back to the first hole and start over. Continue drill until you can finish without leaving a putt short and yet never having worse than a two putt.

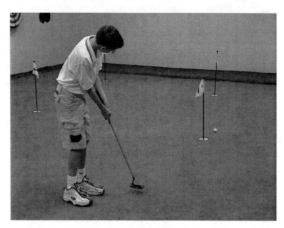

- **Chipping over a bag Drill**—This drill is designed to help the student learn to trust the loft of the club and learn not to help the ball into the air. Place your golf bag at the edge of the practice green between you and the hole. Practice chipping balls over the bag and allowing them to roll to the hole. Place the ball about 4-feet behind the bag and use a pitching wedge to chip the ball; do not pitch it.

Name _____   Section _____

Chapter Eight Review

1. What is often referred to as the most overused club in the bag? _____

2. What is the second most overused club in the bag? _____

3. The short game can represent what portion of the overall game, especially for beginners? _____

4. What is the simplest stroke in golf? _____

5. Which shot is more predictable, the chip shot or the pitch shot? _____ Why?

   _____

   _____

6. What three factors are instrumental in developing a good short game?

   _____

   _____

7. What is a great way to develop feel? _____

   _____

8. List four factors that affect the type of shot you choose to play? _____

   _____

   _____

   _____

9. When faced with a tight lie you should use a club with more or less loft?

   _____

10. Adding emotion usually does what to potential? _____

CHAPTER NINE

PUTTING

The Mechanics of Putting

It is difficult to say that there is a right way or a wrong way to putt. There are as many different putting styles on the tour as there are players. The truth is putting is very individualized. Some players set up to the ball very tall like Ben Crenshaw while others set up to the ball very bent over like Jack Nicklaus. There are those who have closed stances like Arnold Palmer and those who prefer a square stance like that of Tiger Woods. Certain players use long putters like Rocco Mediate while others prefer very short putters like Ken Green. Although there are a number of different approaches to putting, there are certain fundamentals that when present seem to produce more consistency.

There are basically four fundamentals, which I feel should be present regardless of the putting style you adopt.

1. *Develop a comfortable and repeatable setup.* The only way to become a good putter is to practice. Practice is extremely difficult if you are not comfortable. And the success of any stroke relies on its ability to be accurately repeated. Consistency is the key to success.

2. *Position yourself to the ball in such a way as to always have your eyes slightly inside the ball.* Looking down one line while trying to putt down another is simply asking for problems.

3. *Develop a pendulum stroke that utilizes the large muscles and keeps the smaller muscles like those in the wrist passive.* Smaller muscles, like those in the wrist, are much harder to control than the larger muscles in the back. Using the wrists to stroke the putt allows the putter face to open and close thru the ball, while using the back muscles allow the wrists to stay passive thus keeping the putter face square thru impact.

4. ***Always accelerate with rhythm.*** Deceleration results in the putter face closing as well as reduces the odds of putting a true roll on the ball. Taking the putter back to slow and then rushing the down stroke is not the proper way to accelerate. The backstroke and the down stroke should be very similar in speed with the down stroke gradually picking up speed thru the ball.

The Grip

The search for the perfect grip has led to the development of a number of very unique grips. When choosing a grip keep in mind the important role the grip plays in developing a good putting stroke. It must keep the clubface square throughout the stroke **and it must be comfortable.** Once a grip is chosen stick with it. Each time you grip the putter make sure the grip is exactly the same. Pay close attention to detail; consistency is the key to developing a fundamentally sound stroke. Figure 9.1 contains examples of the different grips used today.

Reverse Overlap   Cross Hand   The Claw   Split Hand

Figure 9.1

The Posture

Posture as stated earlier in this chapter is a matter of preference. It is highly recommended that you experiment with different posture positions until you find one that is comfortable and easy for you to repeat. Remember in choosing a posture position it is important to set your eyes over the ball. Figure 9.2 contains examples of the different putting styles used today.

  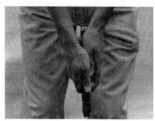

Belly Putter   Long Putter   Conventional

Figure 9.2

Alignment and Ball Position

There are three basic ways one can align themselves to their target; they may be open, square, or closed (see figure 9.3). Open alignment is where the feet are aligned left of the target line. Square alignment is where the feet are aligned parallel to the target line, and closed alignment is where the feet are aligned right of the target line. Although there are tour players who use each of these methods it is highly recommended that a square alignment be used (see figure 9.4).

The correct ball position is also left up to the preference of the student although it is highly recommended that the ball be played slightly forward of center. The ball being played too far forward will result in pulled shots whereas the ball being played too far back will result in pushed shots. The ball position will tend to be farther back in the stance with an opened stance and farther forward with a closed stance.

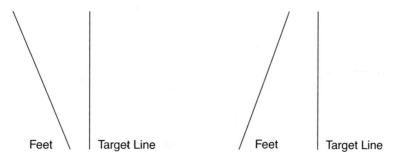

Feet | Target Line   Feet | Target Line

Figure 9.3

Figure 9.4

Square Stance

The Putting Stroke

The putting stroke is the simplest stroke in golf. It is basically a pendulum stroke involving the arms and the large muscles in the back. The lower body is stationary and the wrists should remain firm. **The tempo of the stroke should remain constant with a slight increase in speed from the ball forward towards the target.** As a general rule of thumb the longer the putt the longer the putting stroke, the shorter the putt the shorter the putting stroke. In other words it should take the same amount of time for the putter to swing back and through for a 5' putt as it would for a 50' putt. Visible increases in speed are generally a sign of a poor putter.

Imagine a triangle formed by the two arms and a line across the shoulders. This imaginary triangle should stay intact and swing back and through the stroke as if it were a pendulum (see figure 9.5). The lower body should remain still, the head should remain still and the wrists should stay firm throughout the shot.

Figure 9.5

Reading the Greens

Reading the greens is much more difficult today than in the past. Greens were built in such a way that they would drain towards natural ditches and lakes. One could always depend on the putt to break towards those areas. Modern courses are built with sophisticated drainage systems, which allow greens to be constructed with any design imaginable. To be a successful putter one must be able to read greens. There are two factors to holing putts. One must roll the ball on the correct line to the hole and two the ball must be rolling the correct speed. If you are wrong on either of these factors the ball will not go in the hole. It is therefore important that you know what to expect before you putt the ball. Learning to read greens is just that; it is learned. The more experience you have the more proficient you will become.

Direction as well as speed must be taken into consideration as well as judged properly if a putt is to be holed.

There are several factors, which can determine the speed, and the amount of break a putt will have:

1. The slope or the **undulation** (changes in elevation of the green) is perhaps the most telling sign of the speed and break that a putt will take on. **Up hill will slow putts down while downhill will speed putts up.** An elevation higher on the left will cause a putt to break right just as an elevation higher on the right will cause a putt to break left.

2. Grain also affects the speed and direction of the putt. Grain is basically the direction the grass is leaning and can change throughout the day. Auxins in the stems of grass move away from sunlight so as to cause the side of the stem towards the sunlight to become weaker and lean in that direction. Therefore as the sun moves across the sky the grain can actually change throughout the day. **A putt into the grain will be much slower whereas a putt down grain will tend to have more speed.** A good way to tell which way the grain is running is to look at the grass in the direction of the putt, then turn and look in the direction away from the putt. Down grain will always have a shinier appearance and into the grain will always appear duller. **Grain running left to right will cause the putt to break right while grain running right to left will cause the putt to break left. When playing a breaking putt play a straight putt and allow the break to move the ball to the hole (see figure 9.6).**

Figure 9.6

3. The height at which the grass is cut will also affect the speed of the putt. The taller the grass the slower the putt, the shorter the grass the faster the putt. The shorter the grass the less the ball will break. The taller the grass the more the ball will break.

As you approach the green look to see if you can get an idea of the elevation changes, if any, between your ball and the hole. Before putting walk around the putt and look at it from several different angles. Try to determine if it is up hill or down hill, side hill or flat. Look at the grain to see if it is with your putt or against. Try to determine what effect it may have on the direction of the putt if any. Take one last look from behind your ball down the line, organize the information and use it to help you decide the direction and speed needed to hole the putt (see figure 9.7). Then **commit to your decision and confidently roll the ball into the hole.**

Figure 9.7

Some Do's and Don'ts

Do's

- Develop a comfortable setup
- Position your eyes over the ball
- Develop a pendulum stroke using the large muscles in the back
- Always accelerate thru the ball
- Spend time learning to read the greens
- Practice, especially the short putts

- Be consistent with the setup as well as the stroke.
- **Develop and use a routine**

Don'ts

- Choose a setup and a stroke simply because your favorite tour pro putts that way
- Spend more time practicing long putts than practicing short ones
- Dramatically vary the speed of your backstroke and your down stroke
- Use the wrists to stroke the ball
- Look up before you stroke through the ball
- Try to guide the ball to the hole
- **Decelerate through the ball**

Drills

- <u>Straw Drill</u>—This drill is designed to teach the student not to look up or 'peek' until the putt is away. Place a straw in your mouth and point it at the ball. Stroke the putt while continuing to keep the straw pointing to where the ball originally lay. Don't look but listen for the putt to drop. Five feet is a good distance for this drill.

- **The Acceleration drill**—This drill is designed to help the student develop a feel for accelerating through the putt. Take a normal stance and place the putter behind the ball. Without taking a backswing push the ball forward to the hole. Use this drill from a distance of about three feet. After you feel comfortable, try taking a short backswing 3-4 inches and accelerate thru the ball from the same distance.

- **Look at the hole drill**—This drill is designed to help free up your putting stroke and teach you to swing the club as opposed to hitting at the ball. Address the ball and assume your normal setup. Turn your head slightly and focus your eyes on the hole. Make a putting stroke thru the ball towards the hole while maintaining eye contact with the hole. This drill is most effective when used from 10-20 feet.

- **Three-foot point drill**—This drill is designed to help the student focus when practicing putting short putts. From a distance of about 3 feet putt balls into the hole until you reach a score of 30. You earn a point for every putt you make, deduct 3 points for every putt you miss, and deduct 5 points for every putt you leave short. When you become proficient at this drill back up to a distance of 5 feet and do the same.

Name _____   Section _____

Chapter Nine Review

1. List the four basic fundamentals of putting. _____

_____

_____

2. How would you describe an alignment that has the feet aiming right of the target line?

_____

3. Describe the tempo of the putting stroke. _____

_____

4. What are the two factors necessary to hole a putt? _____

_____

5. List two factors that affect the speed of a putt? _____

and _____

6. List two factors that affect the direction of a putt. _____

and _____

7. When playing a breaking putt you should always play a straight putt and allow the break to move the ball to the hole. True or False _____

8. After gathering all the information about the putt you're faced with you should

_____

9. Should your lower body remain still throughout the putting stroke or should your head remain still throughout the stroke? _____

10. List three putting don'ts described in this chapter. _____

_____

_____

_____

CHAPTER TEN

CHIPPING AND PITCHING

The Chip Shot

The chip shot is a one-lever stroke, which is a very simple yet quite effective shot. Learning to chip properly is simply a matter of choosing the right club and practicing. In choosing the club remember to let the lie dictate the shot. Always use only enough loft to carry the ball to the putting surface and allow the ball to roll to the hole. As a rule the closer to the green you are the less loft you use. Avoid chipping with lofted clubs when at all possible. The mechanics necessary to chip effectively are very easy to learn. The feel required to be a good chipper however, will have to be developed through practice. **A chip shot is simply a putt with a club other than a putter.** To set up to a chip shot properly is much more difficult than the shot itself.

First align yourself left (open to your target) of the target about 30 degrees (see figure 10.1). This allows the lower body to be out of the way as well as provides a better view of the target line. Play the ball back of center in your stance, keep the feet close together, and keep more weight on the left side than the right (see figure 10.1). Make sure you are close enough to the ball to allow the eyes to be directly over the ball. This allows you to

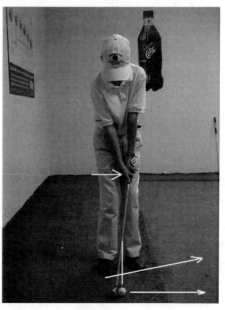

Figure 10.1

Figure 10.2

look down the same line as that which your club will be traveling on as opposed to looking down a skewed line inside of your target line (see figure 10.2). Choke down on the club so as to have better feel and at the address position make sure the hands are in front of the ball (see figure 10.1). Play the shot the same as you would a putt, using a pendulum stroke. Try to keep the speed of the backswing and the downswing consistent. Changing the speed of the downswing will usually result in poor distance control. Keep the wrists passive and use the arms as a unit swinging the club back and thru with the big muscles in the upper back. Never try to help the ball into the air but rather allow the loft of the club to do so.

Some Do's and Don'ts

Do's

- Always let the lie dictate the shot
- Use as little loft as possible
- Setup properly
- Use no wrists
- Remember it is a putt with a club that's not a putter

Don'ts

- Try to lift the ball into the air
- Vary the speed of the swing back and thru
- Use more loft than necessary to carry the ball to the green.

Drills

The long club drill is a very effective drill when trying to develop the proper feel of a chip shot. Take a shaft or another club and place it along side your 7-iron in such a way that the club extends up and past the grip of the 7-iron (see figure 10.3). When gripping the two clubs together make sure

Figure 10.3

the extended club runs along your left side and under your left arm. Chip balls trying not to let the club hit your left side at impact. If it does you're using your wrists to make the shot and not the arms as a unit.

The Pitch Shot

Pitching the ball is usually viewed as a two-lever stroke. The wrists are the second lever and are used to help generate club head speed. This speed, along with added loft, causes the ball to rise quickly and sit softly on the green. The pitch shot is an important shot to learn; it is however too often over used. Pitching the ball is a lot less consistent than chipping the ball and requires much more feel. **The pitch shot should only be used when a chip shot absolutely will not work.**

The setup is very similar to that of the chip shot. The ball will be played slightly more forward and you will be a bit farther away from the ball. Unlike the chip shot, the wrists will hinge slightly on the backswing thus allowing the club head to go farther back (see figure 10.4). The most important thing to remember about pitching the ball is to always accelerate thru the ball. Failure to do so will result in fat and thin shots.

Pitching the ball requires a much better lie than does chipping. Remember to let the lie dictate the shot. Like with most shots in golf, the key to success is your confidence in the shot. Spend ample time practicing this shot before you try to use it on the course. When you decide to pitch the ball commit to that decision and be aggressive. **Lack of commitment to a shot will result in fear and fear results in tension.** To be successful pitching the ball your hands and arms must be relaxed. Last but not least always allow the loft of the club to get the ball into the air, never help it. Always hit down and thru the ball.

Some Do's and Don'ts

Do's

- Chip whenever possible
- Accelerate thru the ball
- Commit to the shot
- Stay relaxed

Don'ts

- Decelerate thru the shot
- Try to help the ball into the air
- Pitch from a very poor lie
- Take the club away flat and to the inside

Figure 10.4

- Hit the shot without being committed to it
- Always hit down and thru the ball

Drills

Drop the arms drill—This is a great drill for helping you learn to swing the club as opposed to trying to lift the ball. Set up to the ball properly and with a slight rotation to the right in the backswing, work the club up to a position about waist high with the wrists partially hinged. Begin the downswing by a rotation into the left side and drop the arms and the club thru the ball. Focus should be placed on a spot twelve inches past the ball and try to go to that spot on the downswing.

Quarter drill—This drill can help you develop the feel for the short pitch shot, a shot used when relatively close to the green. Set up to the ball properly and with a slight rotation to the right in the backswing, work the club up to a position about waist high with the wrists partially hinged. Swing down and thru the ball towards the target but stop the club about the 4 o'clock position on the follow-through. At this point check to see if the clubface is in a position to allow a quarter to be laid on the face without falling to the ground.

This is a great way to learn to keep the hands passive thru the shot. The finish position can only be obtained if the club remains square thru the impact area. When done properly the result will be a lofted shot that will sit softly, great for around the green.

Name _____   Section _____

Chapter Ten Review

1. Describe a chip shot. _____

   _____

2. Where should the ball be played in your stance when chipping?

   _____

3. Where should your hands be in relationship to the ball when chipping?

   _____

4. Where should your alignment be in relationship to the target line when chipping?

   _____

5. What dictates the type of shot you're going to hit? _____

6. What is the difference between a chip and a pitch? _____

   _____

   _____

7. When should a pitch shot be used? _____

8. What is the most important thing to remember when pitching the ball?

   _____

9. Lack of commitment to a shot will result in what? _____

   _____

10. List three don'ts when chipping. _____

    _____

    _____

CHAPTER ELEVEN

HITTING TROUBLE SHOTS

Hitting Trouble Shots

The best way to teach someone to get out of trouble is to first teach him or her how to avoid it. Play smart, avoid your weaknesses and play to your strengths. If playing from the sand is a problem for you then choose a club that will take the sand out of play. Although the above is great advice it is inevitable that sooner or later you will find yourself in a bad spot. All golfers regardless of their skill level from time to time find themselves in a less than an admirable position. Understanding how to play from these positions can lower your scores dramatically. Below are several situations you may find yourself in as well as a way to get out of them.

Playing from the Rough

The key to playing from the rough is choosing the right club. The lie will dictate what club you can use. Too often golfers choose the club due to the distance they are from the green. This is often the worst thing you can do when faced with a shot from the rough. Thick rough will catch the clubface and slow it down as well as cause it to shut through impact. A ball therefore sitting down in thick rough may only be able to be advanced a short distance. The best way to approach this situation is to use a club with plenty of loft and a relatively steep swing and play the ball back to the fairway. A ball sitting up in the rough that can be struck cleanly can result in what is known as a flier. A flier is a ball that travels much farther than expected. Fliers are a result of a lack of backspin being put on the ball due to the grass that is between the ball and the face of the club, at impact. Identifying this situation and choosing the proper club will alleviate many costly mistakes.

Playing from the Woods

It has been said that a tree is 90% air; so is a screen door. A ball will not pass thru a screen door and the results are similar when trying to hit a ball thru a tree. Too often golfers try shots out of the woods that are simply impossible. Perhaps the shots are not impossible, but certainly improbable. If the skill required to execute such a miraculous shot were present in the golfer he or she would not be in the woods. Quite simply put **choose a path of least resistance and put the ball back in play.**

Fade Shots

Causing the ball to purposely move from right to left is certainly an advantage at times. The best way to do this is to change the setup not the swing. Align to the left of the target approximately where you want the ball to start out. Next align your clubface at the target or where you want the ball to finish. Finally make a normal swing down the new setup alignment and simply allow the ball to move due to the open clubface and the path of the club.

Hooks Shots

Causing the ball to purposely move from left to right is certainly an advantage at times. The best way to do this is to change the setup not the swing. Align to the right of the target approximately where you want the ball to start out. Next align your clubface at the target or where you want the ball to finish. Finally make a normal swing down the new setup alignment and simply allow the ball to move due to the closed clubface and the path of the club.

Sand Shots

Playing from the sand is much easier than it appears. Remember that when in the sand you may not ground your club; if you do so it is a 2-stroke penalty. Set up to the ball slightly open to your target. Work your feet firmly into the sand so as to ensure good footing. Grip the club with the face about 45 degrees open and play the ball a bit forward in the stance (see figure 11.1). Make a swing down the line of your feet. Strike the sand behind the ball and allow the sand between the clubface and the ball to get the ball out of the sand trap. The amount of sand between the clubface and the ball varies with how far behind the ball you hit. A good rule of thumb is to pretend the ball is on a tee. If the situation requires a soft short sand shot, (try saying that quickly), then pick the club up quickly during the backswing and imagine swinging the club thru the tee breaking it in half on the downswing. If the situation requires a longer sand shot then take the club back with a wider and more shal-

Figure 11.1

long sand shot

short sand shot

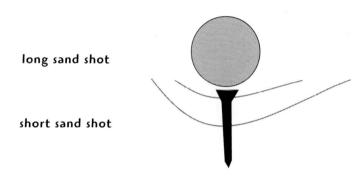

Figure 11.2

low arc during the backswing and imagine swinging the club thru the tee breaking it close to the top on the downswing. As a rule the closer to the top of the imaginary tee you hit, the farther the ball will carry and roll, the closer to the bottom of the tee you hit the shorter the ball will carry and roll (see figure 11.2). The sand will cause the club to slow down dramatically so be sure to **always accelerate thru the ball;** problems arise when you decelerate due to a fear of hitting the ball too far.

Playing from Uneven Lies / Uphill-Downhill-Sidehill Lies

Playing from uneven lies requires a slightly different setup and club selection than does normal lies.

- Uphill lies—When you are faced with an uphill lie try to set your shoulders parallel to the lie of the ground. Play the ball forward in your stance and be sure to take more club than you normally need for that distance. Due to the lie and the setup a 7-iron for example becomes a 9-iron. (See figure 11.2)

- Downhill lies—When you are faced with a downhill lie try to set your shoulders parallel to the lie of the ground. Play the ball back in your stance and be sure to take less club than you normally need for that distance. Due to the lie and the setup a 7-iron for example becomes a 5-iron. (See figure 11.2)

- Side hill lies—
  1. When the ball is above your feet choke down on the club and play for the shot to draw slightly, aim right. The ball will have a tendency to draw due to the club being in a more upright position. The heel will usually catch first and cause the club to close.

2. When the ball is below your feet play for the shot to fade slightly, aim left. The ball will have a tendency to fade due to the club being in a more flat position. The toe will usually catch first and cause the club to open.

Playing Wind Shots

When playing in the wind club selection becomes extremely important. Many amateurs try to hit the ball harder into the wind and in doing so place much more backspin on the ball causing it to rise more and the shot to be even shorter of target. Never try to overpower the ball into or even downwind. Allow the stance to become slightly wider and move the weight a bit more into the left side at the address position. When playing into the wind or downwind choose plenty of club and focus on making a smooth rhythmic swing thru the ball. Advanced players may choose to lower the trajectory of their shots by playing the ball more back in the stance. This is usually not a good idea for beginners who are much better served by simply choosing more club and making a smooth controlled swing.

Figure 11.3

Chapter Eleven Review

1. What is the first thing to consider when faced with a shot from the rough?

   _____

2. A ball sitting down in the rough requires what type of shot?

   _____

   _____

   _____

3. A ball sitting up in the rough can produce what type of shot?

   _____

4. What is the best course of action when playing from the woods?

   _____

5. How does the alignment and clubface vary when hitting an intentional fade?
   Alignment _____ Clubface _____

6. How does the alignment and clubface vary when hitting an intentional draw?
   Alignment _____ Clubface _____

7. Should more or less sand be taken when trying to hit a soft short bunker shot?

   _____

8. When you are faced with a downhill shot should you use more or less club than
   normal? _____

9. When faced with a side hill lie, which places the ball below your feet, the ball will
   have a tendency to go which way? _____

10. What causes a ball to go higher and shorter when hitting into the wind and why?

    _____

    _____

    _____

CHAPTER TWELVE

COMMON SWING FAULTS

In this chapter we will look at the most common swing faults and talk briefly about their causes and how to fix them. **Remember all swing faults are a result of poor fundamentals.** Playing throughout the seasons can cause you to pick up bad habits. After prolonged play in the wind for example, the stance will tend to widen and the weight will tend to move too much forward. Periodically it is advised that you review the fundamentals and make sure they are still in place.

Hitting the Ball "Thin"

Hitting the ball thin is what happens when the club makes contact with the center of the ball (see figure 12.1). This error is usually a result of inappropriate movement during the golf swing. This movement may be due to: (1) a rising up of the upper body through impact, (2) too much lateral motion with the upper or the lower body on the downswing or, (3) the hips trying to rotate too quickly. Lets take a look individually at each one of these causes:

Figure 12.1

- **A rising of the upper body through impact.**

  Cause—This is most always a result of poor posture at the setup position. For example too much or not enough bend in the knees, an arched spine, and a setup that is too close or too far from the ball all result in a rising and a lowering of the upper body throughout the swing

Figure 12.2

Cure—To cure this problem simply work on your posture and your overall setup at address. Try to rotate around your spine.

- **Too much lateral motion with the upper or the lower body on the downswing**

  Cause—This can often be caused by improper leg action, a poor weight shift, or inappropriate head movement. A collapsed left knee at the top of the backswing can allow the upper body to fall forward to begin the downswing. An improper weight shift such as a reverse pivot (see figure 12.3) can cause the lower body to move forward and the upper body to move backwards during the downswing.

  Cure—Solidify the lower body during the golf swing. Maintain the same amount of flex in both legs during the backswing, and work into a firm left leg during the downswing. Make sure the weight moves properly into the right side during the backswing so it can move properly into the left side during the downswing. To do this you must allow the head to move slightly to the right during the backswing while rotating the hips. **The head does not remain still but must be allowed to move to the right in the swing.**

Figure 12.3

- **The hips trying to rotate too quickly.**

  Cause—This movement is simply a result of trying to overpower the ball, trying to hit it too hard, or a misunderstanding of the role the hips play in the downswing (see figure 12.4).

  Cure—**Make it a point to never hit the ball with more than an 80% of maximum speed swing.** Each club will hit the ball a specific distance when struck properly; accept it and try to hit the ball that specific distance. If the ball needs to go farther than you can hit it with that club, change clubs. If you run out of clubs change tees.

Figure 12.4

Hitting the Ball "Fat"

Hitting the ball fat is what happens when the club strikes the ground before it strikes the ball (see figure 12.5). This is usually a result of inappropriate movement or overactive hands during the golf swing. This movement may be due to dropping the upper body through impact, improper lateral motion with the lower body on the downswing, or the hands releasing too quickly. Let's take a look individually at each one of these causes:

- **A lowering of the upper body through impact.**

  Cause—This is most always a result of poor posture at the setup position, for example, too much or not enough bend in the knees, an arched spine, and a setup that is

Figure 12.5

Figure 12.6

too close or too far from the ball all result in rising and lowering the upper body throughout the swing (see figure 12.6).

Cure—To cure this problem simply work on your posture and your overall setup at address.

- **Improper lateral motion with the lower body on the downswing.**

  Cause—Remaining on your right side on the downswing and not being able to rotate are usually a result of an improper weight shift.

  Cure—Solidify the lower body during the golf swing. Maintain the same amount of flex in both legs during the backswing and work into a firm left leg during the down-

swing (see figure 12.7). During the backswing feel as though you had a volleyball between your knees. Make sure the weight moves properly into the right side during the backswing so it can move properly into the left side during the downswing. To do this you must allow the head to move slightly to the right during the backswing while rotating the hips. **The head does not remain still but must be allowed to move**

Figure 12.7   **to the right in the swing.**

- **The hands releasing too quickly.**

  Cause—The hands releasing too quickly is usually a result from a need to catch up in the downswing or a desire to hit the ball, as opposed to swinging the club through the ball (see figure 12.8). This need to catch up with the arms is caused by, more than anything else, an improper weight shift. The weight is working backwards away from the ball or the weight is already past the ball.

  Cure—Learn the proper weight shift as explained in chapter 5. Always focus on swinging the club as opposed to hitting the ball. Maintaining wrist cock, not losing it, is what enables us to hit the ball farther. **Relax the hands and swing the club.**

Figure 12.8

Slicing

A slice is a result of an outside-to-inside swing path with an open clubface. Slicing the ball is a result of the improper swing path and/or clubface position through the impact area. There are a number of reasons why one might slice the golf ball. An incorrect grip, poor posture, an improper weight shift, and faulty alignment are all factors in slicing the ball.

- **An incorrect grip.**

  Cause—Not learning the proper grip results in a multitude of swing errors. If the grip is too weak (see figure 12.9), the face of the club will be open at impact. This results in shots going right, which causes students to aim more left, resulting in an outside-to-in swing path with an open clubface—a slice.

  Cure—Learn to grip the club properly, see chapter 5.

Figure 12.9

- **Poor posture.**

  Cause—Poor posture can lead to an up and down motion in the swing, which can result in a lack of rotation. This lack of rotation can, and most often does, result in a picking up of the club. When this occurs the first move down is forward with the left shoulder, which causes the arms to move outward (see figure 12.10). Outside in swings can result in a slice.

  Cure—Develop good posture, see chapter 5.

- **An improper weight shift.**

  Cause—An improper weight shift, such as a reverse pivot can cause the club to work inside on the backswing (see figure 12.3). This will most always result in an outside-in downswing path.

Figure 12.10

Cure—Learn to shift the weight properly. The weight must move into the right side on the backswing if it is to move into the left side on the downswing. Focus on turning into the right knee while the upper body is rotating around the spine. Allow the head to move slightly to the right while making sure the hips do not move laterally during the backswing.

- **Faulty alignment.**

  Cause—Poor alignment causes a golfer to make bad swings in general. Aiming right but trying to swing at a target to the left will result in an outside-to-in swing path.

  Cure—Work on lining up properly by placing a club on the ground behind the ball pointing at your target. Then place another club parallel to that club where your feet are. Practice this on the range until the aim of your club and where you are looking are the same.

Figure 12.11

Hooking

A hook is the result of an inside-to-outside swing path with a closed clubface. Hooking the ball is caused by an improper swing path and or clubface position through the impact area. There are a number of reasons why one might hook the golf ball. An incorrect grip, poor posture, an improper weight shift, and faulty alignment are all factors related to hooking the ball.

- **An incorrect grip.**

  Cause—Not learning the proper grip results in a multitude of swing errors. If the grip is too strong the face of the club will be closed at impact (see figure 12.12). This results in shots going left which causes students to aim more right, which results in an inside-to-outside swing path with a closed clubface—a hook.

  Cure—Learn to grip the club properly, see chapter 5.

Figure 12.12

- **Poor posture.**

  Cause—Poor posture can lead to an up and down motion in the swing, which can result in a lack of rotation. This lack of rotation can and most often does result in a picking up of the club. When this occurs the first move down for some is a dropping of the right shoulder and the arms as well as a falling back of the upper body. Thus an inside-to-outside swing path occurs. Inside-to-outside swings can result in a hook.

  Cure—Develop good posture, see chapter 5.

Figure 12.13

- **An improper weight shift.**

  Cause—An improper weight shift such as a slide can cause the club to be picked up on the backswing (see figure 12.14). This sometimes can result in a dropping under of the right shoulder and arms during the downswing and an inside-out downswing path.

  Cure—Learn to shift the weight properly. The weight must move into the right side on the backswing if it is to move into the left side on the downswing. Focus on turning into the right knee while the upper body is rotating around the spine. Allow the head to move slightly to the right while making sure the hips do not move laterally during the backswing.

Figure 12.14

- **Faulty alignment.**

  Cause—Poor alignment causes a golfer to make bad swings in general. Aiming left but trying to swing at a target to the right will result in an inside-to-outside swing path.

Cure—Work on lining up properly by placing a club on the ground behind the ball pointing at your target. Then place another club parallel to that club where your feet are. Practice this on the range until the aim of the club and where you are looking are the same.

Shanking

Just hearing the word shank can cause more swing faults than one might imagine. A shank occurs when the hosel of the club makes contact with the ball before the face of the club has a chance to do so. Shanking the golf ball is a result of being too close to the ball at impact due to a number of reasons such as a poor setup, bad hand position at impact, or an improper club path.

- **Poor setup.**

  Cause—The most common reason is having too much weight in the heels at the address position while setting up too close to the ball (see figure 12.15). The weight has a tendency during the backswing to move more onto the balls of the feet causing you to be closer to the ball at impact.

  Cure—Develop the proper setup position, see chapter 5. A good drill is to try hitting balls with the heels off the ground. This drill will help you get your weight centered on the balls of your feet.

Figure 12.15

- **Bad hand position at impact.**

  Cause—Trying to lead with the butt of the club causing the clubface to be open and the hosel to approach the ball (see figure 12.16).

  Cure—Practice trapping the ball to learn the proper impact position of the hands; see the trap drill in chapter 5.

Figure 12.16

- **Improper club path.**

  Cause—A poor club path can result in the club approaching the ball too much from the inside or too much from the outside (see figure 12.17). These extreme paths can lead to the hosel hitting the ball first.

  Cure—Learn to swing the club around the spine. Never try to force the club into a position. Make good rotations, both in the backswing and the downswing allowing the arms to swing freely around the torso.

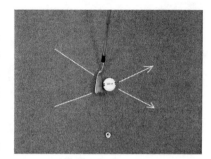

Figure 12.17

Name _____   Section _____

Chapter Twelve Review

1. What are three reasons why one might hit a ball thin?

   _____

   _____

   _____

2. What are three reasons why one might hit a ball fat?

   _____

   _____

   _____

3. What is the culprit behind all swing errors? _____

4. What two things are responsible for a ball slicing or hooking?

   _____

5. What position is the clubface in at impact when the ball is?

   sliced _____hooked_____

6. What is the path of the club thru impact when the ball is?

   sliced _____hooked_____

7. Define a shank. _____

   _____

8. What can cause a shank? _____

   _____

9. What is the cure for being to close to the ball at impact? _____

   _____

10. What swing fault can result from faulty alignment? _____

   _____

CHAPTER THIRTEEN

MENTAL ASPECTS OF THE GAME

Mentally Involved

Many different ingredients are needed to become a successful golfer. In this book we have discussed the importance of developing a golf swing that is mechanically sound by learning and practicing good fundamentals. We have discussed the importance of getting fit with the proper equipment. In the next chapter we will discuss the importance of getting, as well as staying fit physically. All the pieces are in place with the exception of one. A friend of mine, Dr. David Cook, once made a statement that I felt was so profoundly important I have based every aspect of my teachings around it. **"Every voluntary muscle movement begins with a thought"**. That statement opened my eyes to perhaps the single most important fundament in golf, and yet I had never even given it a thought. Dr. Cook followed that statement with one that has had even a greater impact on my teachings, **"we have the ability to control that thought"**.

The argument has always been made that golf is more physical in the beginning and becomes more mental as you advance. The truth is from the very beginning, the first time you pick up a club, golf is 100% mental. **The mindset that we have in learning is as important as the mindset we have in performing.** As Dr. Cook said, we can control that, and controlling it is something we must do from the beginning. Controlling the way you think can greatly increase the rate at which you learn, as well as provide the foundation necessary to become a successful player. To understate the importance of becoming **mentally fit** would be a rules infraction punishable by a lifetime of frustration playing a game that should provide a lifetime of fulfillment.

Tommy Bolt once said "the mind messes up more shots than the body". Tour players have always been aware of the mental aspects of the game but only a few ever came to understand and accept them. None come to mind more than Jack Nicklaus and Tiger

Woods. Tom Layman, a PGA touring professional and winner of 2 majors, when asked of all the players on the tour who he feared most replied "myself". I think if asked the same question both Jack and Tiger would reply "no one". Tiger and Jack are great players because of their sound mindset not in spite of it. **The most influential message you'll ever receive in life comes from yourself.**

Mental Aspects of Learning

The following is an overview of Dr. Cook's approach to the mental aspects of learning and the game. For more information about Dr. Cook and his work please visit—*www.mind setacademy.com.*

Choose to believe in your method—Find *your* swing, not *the* swing.

- Be a student of your game
- Know why you do what you do
- Seek to understand your swing, and then spend your life developing it.
- Establish your foundations
- Don't play a round without them.

Choose positive inner coaching—"To be a great player, you have to be a great coach ... to yourself"

- Our mind communicates to our muscles through words and images.
- Every voluntary muscle movement begins with a thought.
- ... therefore, the origin of every golf swing is in the mind.
- Choose your words carefully; they control the shot.
- You have to take control of your thoughts; be pro-active, know what you are going to think ahead of time.
- *The most influential message you'll ever receive in life comes from yourself.*

Choose to visualize success—"Every shot starts with an empty canvas; it is your task to paint a Picasso. (Johnny Arreaga)

- Images are inevitable: Do you choose to see success or failure?
- Seeing the shot sets the "wheels in motion" for the actual shot.
- Visualizing the shot is a pre-requisite for feeling the shot (i.e. timing, tempo, rhythm).
- Learning takes place when you mentally create the shot.

- At the very least, visualizing is becoming target oriented.
- Choose to see three things as vividly as possible when visualizing:
  1. Aiming point
  2. Shape of shot
  3. Trajectory

Choose to trust your instincts—"Trust is simply the courage to let go and let it happen."

- Trust is letting go of mechanical control. Once you learn to dance you don't count the steps.
- Trust releases instincts; doubt locks them inside.
- Trust is earned by first seeing, then feeling the shot to be made.
- The errors of trust include:
  1. Pressing—increasing the importance of a given shot
  2. Guiding—playing away from trouble rather than to a target
  3. Over aiming—the target becomes too specific, creates tension
  4. Jamming—the mind has too many mechanical thoughts or commands

Choose mental toughness—"Loving to test yourself in the heat of the battle is the seed of a competitive spirit. Consistently putting yourself on the line in competition produces mental toughness.

- Mental toughness is the ability to handle adversity in "the heat of competition" with positive inner coaching.
- Mental toughness is a learned skill.
- Preparing a response ahead of time is the key to responding in the heat of battle.
- We must be prepared for the "realities" of golf. Every shot won't go where we plan for it to go.
- See golf's obstacles as challenges rather than setbacks.
- It is hard to "block out" distractions, but it is relatively simple to replace them.

Choose a pre-shot mindset—"Your number one goal in golf must be to put your mind in position to score over every shot."

- Taking control of the conscious mind puts you in control of your performance.
- Golf is as much a game of overcoming the distractions as it is swinging well.
- Concentration is the focus of attention.

- There are 4 distinct phases of concentration, which must be used over every shot.
  1. Broad External (observe all the variables)
  2. Broad Internal (develop a strategy)
  3. Narrow External (choose a target)
  4. Narrow Internal (focus on one thought as the swing starts)
- Developing a pre shot mindset is the foundation for consistent concentration.
  1. The decision phase
     A) **Observe:** layout, elevation change, yardage, wind, lie, hazards break, grain...
     B) **Strategy:** choose target, type of shot, and club
  2. Shot making phase
     A) **"See it"** paint the shot; see success
     B) **"Feel it"** feel the swing needed to produce the visualized shot
     C) **"Trust it"** this triggers club head movement and the giving up of mechanical control

Choose an effective perspective—"There are no *crucial shots* in the game of golf."

- Golf is a game, not brain surgery.
- Your self worth has nothing to do with the score you post.
- Put your mind in position to score over each shot, then take a "walk in the park" between shots.
- Golf is a privilege; enjoy it.
- Have fun.
- A bad day on the golf course is still better than a good day figuring taxes.

How to Practice

To improve one has to practice. Developing good fundamentals both mentally and physically requires not just practice, but proper practice. For a practice session to be successful two ingredients must be present; the proper mindset and a clear picture as to what is to be accomplished during the session. Simply hitting balls into the range as fast as you can with different clubs will not help you improve your swing, although it may help you become more aerobically fit.

Have a plan when you're practicing both mentally and physically. Entering the practice session with the proper mindset almost assures you of a successful session. Be positive; the learning process is part of the game—enjoy it.

Have a clear picture as to what you're trying to accomplish, how you're going to accomplish it, and how you are going to measure the success of the session. Too often golfers rate a practice session on how well they hit the ball. Working on drills to develop proper mechanics does not always produce good shots. To strike the ball properly requires the mind to be free of mechanical thoughts.

There are basically two types of practice sessions. Practice sessions designed to help you develop better fundamentals, and practice sessions designed to help you free your mind and play the game. When practicing fundamentals mechanics are important and should be the focus of the session. Success is based on the feel you developed during the session, not where the ball goes. Practice sessions designed to free your mind are free of mechanics. The focus is on the routine and the thought process and the ball flight, not mechanics.

Having a routine is important in that it helps to occupy the mind in a positive way. The thought process and ball flight are extremely important. If you cannot develop a clear picture of what you want the ball to do, you will have minimal success. It's difficult to accomplish what you cannot see yourself accomplishing. Mental imagery helps clear the mind of mechanics and gives the brain a good clear picture of the task at hand. Although many may disagree the mental practice is far more rewarding than the mechanical one.

Things that are difficult are only difficult because we choose to see them in that manner. Success is something everyone can experience by simply allowing it to happen. When a student tells me that he or she was scared to hit a specific shot I can't help but wonder what they are afraid of. There is no place for fear in golf—it is a game. Fear causes tension and tension ruins any hopes of having a successful repetitive golf swing. **When faced with a difficult shot one should be excited about the challenge, not afraid of the outcome.**

Learning occurs in four stages. First, you have no idea that you have no idea. This stage is where we all start. It looks simple enough and if he or she can do it, I'm sure that I can. After being frustrated for some time period you reach stage two; you have a very good idea that you had no idea. This is where you come to the conclusion that there is more to it than meets the eye and acknowledge that help is needed.

Next is stage three; you know that you know. In other words you have the knowledge and the skills to accomplish the feat. Finally, comes stage four, you must forget you know and simply do. Most never reach stage four, but choose instead to exist in stage three. Walking is as complicated a movement as the golf swing. Think back to the last lesson you received on how to walk. Once you got the mechanics down, you simply forgot them and began a lifetime of walking successfully, without weekly lessons. Some might say that this is a poor example, that walking is simple, and could be done blindfolded. If you asked those that feel this way to try and walk on a six inch wide board lying on the ground for some distance of thirty feet, their reply would be—no problem. If that board were placed between two buildings some 90 stories tall, their reply would be—no way.

My point is, that walking is walking no matter where you do it. It only becomes difficult when the thought of failure enters the brain. Be positive, enjoy the learning process and then simply play.

The Mental Aspects of Playing

See the fairway not the water. When a negative thought enters your mind replace it with a positive one. This advice is easy to give, but hard to follow. Regardless of what you do you will see the water, and whether you like it or not from time to time negative thoughts will enter your mind. Being prepared is all one can do. Know that each time you play you will be faced with challenges. When they arrive embrace them. If you were perfect the game would be boring. Challenges are why we play in the first place. If a negative thought comes to mind ignore it. Replacing it with a positive one means you just entered into a dialogue with yourself. I'm not sure but I don't think that's healthy and is perhaps illegal in several states. The only reason that thought exists is because you chose to allow it. Fear of failure is not something we are born with; it's something we learn. Juniors have possessed all the best putting strokes I've ever witnessed. I had an 8 year old in my academy who once made 374 three footers without missing for a 75 cent coke. When you tell a 4 year old you'll buy him his favorite toy if he can hit a ball 150 yards in the air, he will spend hours trying to accomplish a feat that we know is impossible. It never crosses his mind that he might not be able to do it. Along the way we lose that "I can do anything attitude" and regardless of how hard we try, we never regain it.

As we grow older we are taught to think logically, be realistic, and to overanalyze ourselves. We judge our every move and place a great deal of emphasis on not making mistakes. **Mistakes are a part of life; if you haven't made one then you've never applied yourself.**

"I missed more than 9,000 shots in my career. I've lost almost 300 games. 26 times I've been trusted to take the game winning shot and missed. I have failed over and over again in my life. And that is why I succeed". Michael Jordan 1998

Perhaps the idea that we can accomplish anything is childish. If so, my advice is to play the game like a child. Be excited by the challenges put before you and eager to show off your skills. Believe that all is possible and—Just Play.

---

*Attitude**

"The longer I live, the more I realize the impact of attitude on life. Attitude, to me, is more important than facts. It is more important than the past, than education, than money, than circumstances, than failures, than successes, than what other people think or say or do. It is more important than appearance, giftedness or skill. It will make or break a company...a church...a home. The remarkable

---

*Charles R. Swindoll, Strengthening Your Grip (Nashville, Tenn.: W Publishing Group, 1982), pp. 206–207. All rights reserved. Used by permission.

thing is that we have a choice everyday regarding the attitude we will embrace for that day. We cannot change our past.... we cannot change the fact that people will act in a certain way. We cannot change the inevitable. The only thing we can do is play on the one string we have, and that is our attitude.... I am convinced that life is 10% what happens to me and 90% how I react to it".

Competitive Golf

Playing the Game

The rules of the game:

1. Always have a procedure to a specific target
2. Play each shot one shot at a time to the best of your ability at that moment
3. When the shot does not please you, forgive and forget, then play the next shot to the best of your ability, at that moment
4. Continue this procedure until all 18 holes are played
5. Post the score
6. After the round, applaud your best efforts, then analyze your mistakes, correct them in your mind, and the round is finished
7. Compare yourself to no one else—only the golfer you know you can be
8. Respect the procedure and post a new score, letting yourself get closer to the edge of your ability

Things to Remember

1. In golf as in life, the attempt to do something in one stroke that needs two strokes is apt to result in taking three.
2. Once you learn to strike the ball, course management and psychology become the dominant factors in successfully playing the game. If you can't manage yourself and the course, you can't play.
3. Golf is a compromise of what your ego wants you to do, what experience tells you to do, and what your nerves will let you do.
4. Competitive golf is played on a five and one half inch course, the space between your ears.
5. Golf is not a game of great shots but one of the most accurate misses. The people who make the smallest mistake wins.

Rules

1. You and only you are responsible for your score, good or bad.
2. Never work on mechanics during a round of golf.
3. At the advanced level the most important aspect of your game is your mental attitude. You must develop a mindset that allows you to be able to concentrate on the task at hand, playing each hole to the best of your ability.
4. In order to accomplish rule 3 you must rid yourself of all feelings that interrupt concentration such as
   - Pride
   - Fear
   - Doubt
   - Hope/Luck

Pride and fear destroy one's ability to think logically. Never be so proud as to play a shot you know that is not logical. Golf is a game, regardless of the outcome life goes on. There is nothing to fear. Never doubt in your ability; trust in yourself and your skills. **THERE IS NO ROOM FOR LUCK.** When you attempt a shot it is not that you hope it will work, but that you know it will work, because you have done it enough to trust it's outcome.

To play golf and be able to score under pressure you must have:

- Simple and easy swing
- Confidence in your short game
- No fear of obstacles

Example: Do not hit an iron, because a fairway has bunkers. Learn to play out of them and the fairway will suddenly appear very wide and your swing will feel freer.

Know your Game

- Your Strengths
- Your weakness

What you cannot do in practice you probably cannot do in competition. You are not playing those that you may be paired with. You are playing the golf course.

Paradoxes of Golf

- To play better, think less.
- To hit it farther, swing easier.
- To gain control, give up control.
- A hard shot requires a soft touch.
- Adding emotions lessens potential.
- When hitting a difficult shot, you play aggressively to a conservative target.
- Short shots cause the highest pressure.
- The goal is simple in golf; the paths are many.
- There is only one target, but many distractions.
- Great swings don't always produce great shots.
- Many times the harder you try the worse it gets.
- Golf is very technical, but must be played very simply.

CHAPTER FOURTEEN

CONDITIONING

It's safe to say many golfers throughout the years have helped to make golf the game it is today. Players like Bobby Jones, Ben Hogan and Bryon Nelson set pretty high standards. Arnold Palmer helped introduce thousands to the sport through his popularity and charisma on television. His style of play and his working class background brought a whole new group of Americans into the game. Perhaps none, however, have helped to grow the sport as much as Tiger Woods. Tiger's passion for winning, his unbelievable heroics, and his ability to make the impossible possible have helped make him one of the most popular athletes of all time. Tiger's not just good for golf, he's good for America. Tiger is the type role model we need; he's a hard worker, a fierce competitor, a gracious loser, and most of all he is who he is, never saying one thing and doing another.

One of the biggest benefits Tiger has brought to the game is his desire to be the best he can be, not just from a golfing standpoint but from a physical standpoint. The great Gary Player promoted being in shape for years, but it was Tiger who made it popular. When asked what advantage he had over the other golfers, his modest answer is, "My physical conditioning." Most touring professionals now make some type of regular exercise a part of their everyday life.

I've always been a fan of those who promote health and well-being. The more physically fit one is, the better one will perform in any sport. Tiger's physical conditioning played a huge role in his winning the 2008 US Open while playing with a broken leg and a torn ACL.

All too often young athletes feel that proper exercise and diet can wait until they're older. Truth is, good health is a lifestyle choice and the choice is much easier to follow if it's made early. It's much the same as a swing flaw, in that the longer you play with it the harder it becomes to change. Young people, for example, can eat poorly and get away with it, but as they age the affects are eventually realized. This discussion of health may seem a bit out of place for a golf book, but remember what I said earlier: **The more physically fit an athlete is, the better he or she will perform.**

Being Physically Fit

Being physically fit doesn't necessarily mean being thin. For example, I was 6' 1" and weighed 160lbs. After a doctor's visit I found out my cholesterol was almost 300, my blood pressure was 140/95, and my heart rate was about 86 bpm. In general, my doctor's assessment was not good. How could this be? I am an athlete and by no means overweight. After being told that a good old-fashioned heart attack was inevitable at the rate I was going, I decided to change directions. First, my eating habits changed dramatically. I gave up the finer cuisines such as colas, pastries, and pizza three times a week, and I began to exercise. I now weigh 180lbs and my vitals are as follows: cholesterol 102, blood pressure 106/69, heart rate 41 bpm. I feel a thousand times better and the doc says I should look into long-term health care—which means I may live long enough to finish this book.

What Does It Mean to be Physically Fit?

Physical fitness is defined as "a set of attributes that people have or achieve that relates to the ability to perform physical activity." In other words, it is more than being able to run a long distance or lift a lot of weight at the gym. Being fit is not defined only by what kind of activity you do, how long you do it, and at what level of intensity. While those are important measures of fitness, they only address single areas. Physical fitness is the body's ability to perform activities without becoming too sore, tired, or getting out of breath. Overall fitness is made up of five main components:

- Cardio respiratory endurance
- Muscular strength
- Muscular endurance
- Body composition
- Flexibility

In order to assess your level of fitness, look at all five components together.

1. What is **cardio respiratory endurance** (cardio respiratory fitness)?

   Cardio respiratory endurance is the ability of the body's circulatory and respiratory systems to supply fuel during sustained physical activity. To improve your cardio respiratory endurance, try activities that keep your heart rate elevated at a safe level for a sustained length of time such as walking, swimming, or bicycling. The activity you choose does not have to be strenuous to improve your cardio respiratory endurance. Start slowly with an activity you enjoy, and gradually work up to a more intense pace.

2. What is **muscular strength?**

   Muscular strength is the ability of the muscle to exert force during an activity. The key to making your muscles stronger is working them against resistance, whether that resistance is from weights or gravity.

3. What is **muscular endurance?**

   Muscular endurance is the ability of the muscle to continue to perform without fatigue. To improve your muscle endurance try cardio respiratory activities such as walking, jogging, bicycling, or dancing.

4. What is **body composition?**

   Body composition refers to the relative amount of muscle, fat, bone, and other vital parts of the body. A person's total body weight (what you see on the bathroom scale) may not change over time. But the bathroom scale does not assess how much of that body weight is fat and how much is lean mass (muscle, bone, tendons, and ligaments). Body composition is important to consider for health and the management of your weight!

5. What is **flexibility?**

   Flexibility is the range of motion around a joint. Good flexibility in the joints can help prevent injuries through all stages of life. If you want to improve your flexibility, try activities that lengthen the muscles such as swimming or a basic stretching program.

Some Benefits of Physical Fitness

- Heart and lungs are stronger
- Cholesterol levels are healthier
- Metabolic rate improves
- More calories are burned and the muscle to fat ratio is better
- Exercise reduces stress
- Exercise causes the body to release endorphins which make you feel better
- Social benefits: you feel better about yourself
- The better you feel about yourself, the higher your confidence level

- Delayed aging process
- Higher fatigue thresholds and greater physical work capacity
- Improved posture and appearance
- Improved neuromuscular skill and physical performance

In general, being physically fit helps you to be the best athlete you can be.

Are You Aerobically Fit?

The next question that you are probably asking yourself is am I aerobically fit? To answer that, go run, walk or crawl, as fast as you can, one and one-half miles (6 laps on a 440 yard track) and compare your result with the following standards: (**Ask your doctor first if you are healthy enough to do so.**)

Table 14.1
One and One-Half Mile Run Norms

	Superior	Good	Fair	Poor	Terrible
Young Golfers (15-25)					
Men					
	Below 9 min.	9-11	11-13	13-15	over 15
Women	11 min.	11-13	13-15	15-16	over 16
Young Adult Golfers (26-35)					
	Below 10 min.	10-12	12-14	14-16	over 16
Women	11 min	11-13	13-16	16-17	over 17
Middle-aged Golfers (36-55)					
	Below 11 min.	11-13	13-15	15-17	over 17
Women	12 min.	12-14	14-16	16-18	over 18
Senior Golfers (56-over)					
	Below 12 min.	12-14	14-16	16-18	over 18
Women	13 min.	13-15	15-17	17-19	over 19

How Can I Get Aerobically Fit?

After completing the one and one-half mile run you will probably realize that you are aerobically unfit, and you may be wondering how you can become fit. To attain maximal benefits from aerobic exercise it is essential to plan a progressive program that meets your specific needs. For example, you may select a program of running, jogging, walking, bicycling, swimming, stationary bicycling, or aerobic dancing. Your selected program should be vigorous enough to tax your heart and regulatory system. No single aerobic exercise is suited to all people because of the tremendous variations in fitness and physical handicaps. The following are some suggestions for selecting an aerobic program:

1. **Identify your fitness needs.** Determine your aerobic fitness level and select a mode of exercise to improve it.
2. **Select a regular time and place for your exercise.**
3. **Do not over-exercise.** This can cause soreness, which will cause you to terminate your exercise program. Approach each exercise session with a positive attitude.
4. **Warm up and cool down before and after each exercise workout.** Approximately two minutes of easy jogging or three minutes of walking should precede an exercise bout to improve blood flow to the heart and muscles. Cooling down or slowly tapering off after exercise is advisable. Never stop exercising abruptly. After a jog or bout of exercise, continue to walk or move around. This allows the blood to return to the heart and not pool in the legs.
5. **Progress slowly.** In exercise, hurrying does not work; it merely invites trouble. Gradually work up to your exercise goals.
6. **Exercise regularly.** Consistency and regularity are necessary for strengthening the CVR system. Spasmodic exercise can be dangerous.
7. **Wear proper shoes.** A poor pair of exercise shoes can cause foot, leg, or hip injuries.
8. **Use caution in hot conditions.** Never exercise vigorously when a combined temperature and humidity reach 165 or above (ie., 85 degrees and 85% humidity).
9. **Get a medical examination, especially if you are over the age of 35.**
10. **Exercise within your tolerance.** Do not push yourself to the extent of becoming overly tired. You should feel refreshed when arising from a night's sleep.

Strength and Muscular Endurance

An exercise program for golfers should include not only CVR training, but muscular strength and endurance training. A distinction between muscle strength and muscle endurance is in order. **Muscle strength** is the ability of the muscle to exert force during an activity. The key to making your muscles stronger is working them against resistance, whether that is from weights or gravity.

Muscular Endurance is the ability of the muscle to continue to perform without fatigue. To improve your muscle endurance, try cardio-respiratory activities such as walking, jogging, bicycling, or dancing. All the major muscles and their movements at each of the major joints involved in the golf swing should be strengthened. The following are some specific strength and endurance exercises that may improve your golf game:

Strength Training

You do not need to have a full complement of gym equipment to train. A pull up bar, which you can buy for about $40, some dumbbells, and an exercise band will be more than enough equipment to help you achieve strength and muscle endurance. Try to perform each strength exercise a minimum of two sets of ten repetitions, three times weekly.

> Push-ups and pull-ups are very effective ways of strengthening the chest, shoulders, back, and arms. Lat, trap, pec, bicep, and triceps muscles are all used in these two exercises. By varying the width and position of the hands you are able to target specific areas of the upper body. These exercises use your own body weight as a form of resistance. Try to focus on form as opposed to quantity while performing these exercises.

Chair dips, barbell curls, shoulder flies, and arm circles are a great way to isolate the triceps and the biceps, as well the delts. Again, form is much more important than quantity

Wall squats, weighted lunges and calf raises are great ways to get the legs in shape.

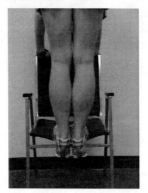

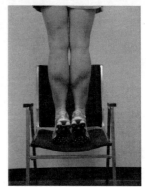

Last but not least, different variations of crunches work wonders in strengthening the core.

Flexibility Exercises

In order to hit the golf ball a greater distance, one must not only develop strength, but flexibility. A lack of flexibility is perhaps the main limiting factor in developing a golf swing. The loss of flexibility is especially evident among adult golfers. Many adult golfers are discouraged by their inability to execute the swing required to become a successful golfer. Research studies have shown that performing specific flexibility exercises will significantly develop flexibility in all the muscles that are required to hit a golf ball properly. Below are some exercises that should be very beneficial to you. These exercises should be done by moving smoothly to the point of stress (avoid bouncing) and holding for eight seconds. Relax and repeat as often as your condition will allow.

Yoga Stretches

Arm and Finger Stretches

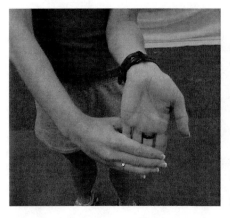

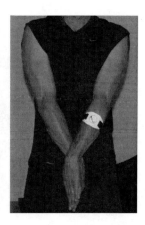

Trunk Stretches

Shoulder Stretches

Hip and Thigh Stretches

Simple Warm-up, Stretch, and Flexibility Exercises

If you commit yourself to warming up effectively, you'll not only have a much better day on the course, you'll be doing a favor to your body by preventing injuries and post-game soreness. So take five minutes and really stretch. You don't need to do anything extraordinary, just the same basic stretches you learned in gym class. Stretch your arms, shoulders, legs, and back. Loosen up your neck. You'll reduce your risk of keeling over on the fourth hole in the middle of a swing, and you won't be nearly as sore the next day. Most elite golfers consider the warm-up a crucial part of their pre-game routine. They feel the warm-up not only helps them physically prepare, but mentally prepare for the round ahead. Warming up can offer a number of physiological and psychological benefits. Physiological benefits of warming up include: increased blood flow to muscles; raising tissue temperature; increased joint range of movement; and elevating heart and metabolic rate. From a psychological perspective, warming-up can form an integral part of the pre-game routine, helping to overcome pre-game tension and assisting the golfer in focusing on the task ahead.

Using a weighted club such as the **Momentus Strength Trainer** to loosen up before a practice session or a round of golf is always a good idea. These clubs are relatively inexpensive and serve as a great way to work out when you're traveling and can't get to a gym or a practice range. Below are a few exercises you can do when you are stuck inside or don't have a chance to visit the gym. These exercises are a great way to increase strength and develop flexibility.

Front Raises (shoulders and back)

Hold the club down in front of you. Keeping your arms straight, slowly raise it up above your head and hold for 2 seconds, then slowly lower it back down. Repeat this drill 12 times.

Side Raises (shoulders)

Hold the club at your side with one hand. Slowly raise it up over your head and hold it for 2 seconds, then slowly lower it back down. Repeat this drill 12 times with each arm.

Forearm Curls (forearms and wrists)

Hold the club down in front of you with your hands on top. Slowly curl it up to your chin and hold for 2 seconds, then slowly lower it back down. Repeat this drill 12 times.

Bicep Curls (forearms and wrists)

Hold the club down in front of you with one hand. Slowly curl it up and hold for 2 seconds, then slowly lower it back down. Repeat this drill 12 times with each arm.

Triceps Extensions (triceps)

Hold the club behind your head with both hands. Keeping your elbows close together, extend it above your head and hold for 2 seconds, then slowly lower it back down. Repeat this drill 12 times.

Summary

Everyone, regardless of skill level, should follow an organized fitness program. Making lifestyle changes such as regular exercise and proper diet are tough, and without an organized plan such changes are almost impossible for the average person. There are many good programs out there. Find one that addresses each area of fitness and lays out a plan for both **exercise** and a proper **diet**. After going it alone for many years without success, I settled on P90X. P90X combines plyometrics, yoga, core synergistics, kenpo, stretching, and weight training. It's a seven days a week program that switches up routines in order to keep the muscles confused. Each aspect of the program targets the above-mentioned areas of fitness. The program helps to build muscle strength, muscle endurance, flexibility, balance, and of course is full of cardio. This program is pretty high impact and not for everyone. It requires a little over an hour per night to be devoted to exercise, and for most of you that's asking too much. Other programs like "Ten Minute Trainer," put out by the same company as P90X, are great for those with little time and those who aren't exactly ready for high impact programs. Remember, the goal is to get fit, not to hurt yourself trying. Diet is by far the hardest part of getting fit. There's just too much good junk food available, and most of us are just too busy to plan out healthy meals. Without proper diet, however, most exercise programs are useless. You need the right fuel in your body to be able to continue to exercise. Otherwise you'll do more harm than good. Once you've settled into a program, you'll start feeling as well as looking better, and you will also start performing better. Your game will improve, I guarantee it; or, you may just keep playing bad. The good news is, you'll probably live a much longer life, thus having more time for lessons!

CHAPTER FIFTEEN

INSTRUCTION

Taking a Golf Lesson

For those who are serious about golf, regardless of their skill level, taking a private lesson should be considered. **It is extremely important to develop good fundamentals early in the learning process.** Some help with the development of these fundamentals can save a student a tremendous amount of time and frustration. Practicing is only beneficial if you are practicing properly. It is not always easy for a student to apply what he or she reads properly or let's say the way the author intended it be applied. As an instructor and an author I understand the challenges students are faced with as well as the challenges authors are faced with and if given a choice I would rather spend an hour with my student as opposed to my student spending an hour with my book.

Technology

As a teaching professional I have spent years trying to find ways to make learning easier for my students. Everyone seems to learn somewhat differently but it has been my experience that the majority of people are visual learners. Allowing a student to actually view their swing and especially a specific area of their swing helps a teacher to get his or her point across more effectively. When a student can view their swing, compare it to another's swing as well as compare the swing they made at the beginning of the lesson with the one they make at the end of the lesson, learning seems to occur more rapidly. This feedback is instrumental in gaining the students confidence. In order for the student to really learn, he or she must believe that the instructor is competent and accurate in diagnosing the problem. If the student leaves the lesson with doubt, they are apt to practice with doubt. **Using video has** allowed me not only to show my students where their problems lie, but also to show them why they are a problem, and how we can overcome them (see figure 15.1).

Digital Coaching Systems

Technology today allows us as instructors to do so much more for our students. With the new video systems we can identify problems quicker, convey the diagnosis in a much clearer manner, and prescribe the work necessary for the student to improve in a way that's very understandable to the student. At my teaching facility we use the V-1 for all individual and group lessons. **The V-1 Digital Coaching System is the most advanced teaching system in use today.** It is the system

Figure 15.1

of choice for such well-known teachers as Butch Harmon and Jim McLean. The V1 Digital Coaching System enables PGA golf professionals such as myself, either in person or via the Internet, to provide the most advanced golf lessons available today. The V1 can capture a golf swing, play it back, analyze it, annotate key parts, compare it to other swings, and record all analysis on a take home DVD. Figures 15.2 and 15.3 are examples of some of the video capabilities of the V1.

The home software version allows me to stay in touch with my students regardless of what school they attend or where they may travel. A student can capture a swing on video and email it to me. I can then analyze the swing and return it to the student within minutes. This is an extremely useful tool considering the number of students I have and the size of the world we live in (see figure 15.4).

Figure 15.2

Figure 15.3

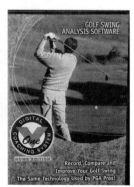

Figure 15.4

How to Take a Lesson

The way in which the student approaches the lesson determines how successful the lesson will be. If it's a quick fix your looking for in most cases you will be somewhat disappointed. The purpose of a golf lesson is to help the student get better. Sometimes that can be accomplished in a reasonably short period of time, sometimes not. More than likely the problem is a result of poor fundamentals and will require some individual practice.

Most students feel they can hit a lot of balls during the lesson and fix their problem on the spot. The reality is that if in the lesson the problem can be identified and the student can gain a good idea of what the problem is, why it's a problem, and how they can begin to fix it, then its been a very successful lesson. Leaving a lesson with a feel for what's right and what's wrong is much more important than leaving a lesson hitting the ball well. **When you are practicing you should be focusing on the areas you're trying to improve, not where the ball is going.**

Below are 10 keys to taking a successful lesson:

- Enter the lesson with an open and positive mindset.
- Express to the instructor what you expect to accomplish from the lesson.
- Be truthful in answering the instructor's questions.
- Make normal swings for the instructor.
- Listen
- Make sure you understand what the instructor has identified as the problem and why it is a problem.
- When you do not totally understand, say so.
- Be clear on what the instructor wants you to work on and why.
- Ask what type of feedback you may expect if practicing properly, improperly.
- Leave the lesson with a plan and stick to it.

If your progress frustrates you remember it took Tiger Woods, who is the best player in the world and works harder than any other player on the tour, almost 13 months to make a simple swing change after winning the 1997 Masters. For you to do so in an hour is perhaps asking a little too much. Be patient and practice properly. Enjoy practicing and you will not only improve but also have fun doing it.

CHAPTER SIXTEEN

GOLF QUOTES, JOKES, AND ANECDOTES

Golf Quotes

The following are a collection of famous golf quotes about this fascinating game:

Golf is an intelligent game, played by intelligent people, stupidly.
    —*The 19th Hole*

If you watch a game, it's fun. If you play it, it's recreation. If you work at it, it's golf.
    —*The 19th Hole*

Golf is a game whose aim is to hit a very small ball into a very small hole, with weapons singularly ill-designed for the purpose.
    —*Winston Churchill*

Golf is a game in which you yell fore, shoot six, and write down five.
    —*Paul Harvey*

Golf is a good walk spoiled.
    —*Mark Twain*

The more I practice, the luckier I get.
    —*Lee Trevino*

I'm going to miss at least seven shots in every 18 holes, so if I'm going to be angry, I might as well start right on the first tee.
    —*Walter Hagen*

If you think it's hard to meet new people, try picking up the wrong golf ball.
—*Jack Lemmon, Actor*

Golf's not that hard. The ball doesn't move.
—*Ted Williams, baseball player*

The definition of pressure in golf is when you play for a five-dollar bet, and you have only two dollars in your pocket.
—*Lee Trevino*

Give me a man with big hands, big feet, and no brains, and I will make a golfer out of him.
—*Walter Hagen*

Give me golf clubs, the fresh air, and a beautiful partner, and you can keep my golf clubs and the fresh air.
—*Jack Benny*

I never pray on the golf course. Actually, the Lord answers my prayers everywhere except on the course.
—*Rev. Billy Graham*

Let's face it, 95 percent of this game is mental. A guy plays lousy golf, he doesn't need a pro, he needs a shrink.
—*Tom Murphy*

Relax? How can anybody relax and play golf? You have to grip the club, don't you?
—*Ben Hogan*

All men are created equal and I am one shot better than the rest.
—*Gene Sarazen*

Golf is an easy game
—It's just hard to play.
—*The 19th Hole*

Water holes are sacrificial waters where you make a steady gift of your pride and high-priced balls.
—*Tommy Bolt*

I would not hurt a chicken crossing the road, but if I got a man in trouble on the golf course I'd kick the hell out of him. I don't care if he's my best friend.
—*Sam Snead*

You have to make corrections in your game a little bit at a time. It's like taking your medicine. A few aspirins will probably cure what ails you, but the whole bottle might just kill you.
—*Harvey Penick*

Mulligan: Invented by an Irishman who wanted to hit one more twenty-yard grounder.
—*Jim Bishop*

The meek shall inherit the earth, but they will never hit a par five green in two.
—*The 19th Hole*

Golf is a game where you have to play your foul balls.
—*Sam Snead*

I was three over—one over the house, one over the patio, and one over the swimming pool.
—*George Brett, Baseball player*

My worst day on the golf course still beats my best day in the office.
—*The 19th Hole*

It's hard to keep score like I do with someone looking over your shoulder.
—*Bob Hope*

Some guys on the tour get so nervous playing for their own money, the greens don't need fertilizing for a year.
—*Dave Hill*

Putting is simple. You need a sound putting stroke, confidence, patience, feel, and visualization.
—*Seve Ballesteros*

Charley hits some good woods—most of them are trees.
—*Glenn Campbell, on his friend Charley Pride*

A golf course is the epitome of all that is purely transitory in the universe, a space not to dwell in, but to get over as quickly as possible.
—*Jean Giraudoux*

Anyone who criticizes a golf course is like a person invited to a house for dinner, who on leaving, tells the host that the food was lousy.
—*Gary Player*

The golfer has more enemies than any other athlete. He has fourteen clubs in his bag, all of them different, eighteen holes to play, all of them different, every week; and all around him are sand, trees, grass, water, wind, and 143 other players. In addition, the game is 50 percent mental, so his biggest enemy is himself.
    —*Dan Jenkins*

If your adversary is a hole or two down, there is no serious cause for alarm in his complaining of a severely sprained wrist. Should he happen to win the next hole, these symptoms will in all probability become less troublesome.
    —*Horace G. Hutchinson*

Golf is not a sport; it is men in ugly pants walking.
    —*Rosie O'Donnell*

It's good sportsmanship to not pick up lost golf balls while they're still rolling.
    —*Mark Twain*

The biggest liar in the world is the golfer who claims he plays the game merely for the exercise.
    —*Tommy Bolt*

Don't blame me. Blame the foursome ahead of me.
    —*Excuse used by men for being late at home*

I call my sand wedge my half-Nelson, because I can always strangle the opposition with it.
    —*Byron Nelson*

Real golfers go to work to relax.
    —*The 19th hole*

Serenity is knowing that your worst shot is still going to be pretty good.
    —*Johnny Miller*

The life of a professional golfer is precarious at best. Win and they carry you to the clubhouse on their shoulders; lose and you pay the caddies in the dark.
    —*Gene Sarazen*

Real golfers have two handicaps, one for bragging' and one for betting.
    —*The 19th Hole*

Golf is like a marriage. However, if I had to choose between my wife and my golf clubs, well, I'd miss her.
    —*The 19th Hole*

Gimme: An agreement between two losers who can't putt.
    —*The 19th Hole*

Golf does strange things to people. It makes liars out of honest men, cheats out of Saints, cowards out of brave men, and fools out of everybody.
  —*Milton Gross, writer*

When baseball players, football players, and hockey players retire, they take up golf. I've never heard of a golfer retiring and taking up hockey. This is the greatest game.
  —*Lee Trevino*

The hardest shot is a one-iron at ninety yards from the green, where the ball has to be played against an oak tree, bounces back into a sand trap, hits a stone, bounces on the green, and then rolls into the cup. That shot is so difficult I have only made it once.
  —*Zeppo Marx*

My putting is so bad I could putt off a table-top and still leave the ball halfway down the leg.
  —*J.C. Snead*

That little white ball won't move until you hit it, and there's nothing you can do after it has gone.
  —*Babe Didrickson Zaharias*

The average golfer doesn't play golf, He attacks it.
  —*Jackie Burke*

Like life, golf can be humbling; however, little good comes from brooding about mistakes we've made. The next shot, in golf or in life, is the big one.
  —*Grantland Rice*

Golf is not a matter of life or death; it's more serious than that.
  —*The 19th Hole*

Golf is another four-letter word.
  —*The 19th Hole*

My old friend Jack Benny, who is notoriously noted for being frugal, has only had one ball all his golfing life. And now he has lost it. The string came off!
  —*Bob Hope*

May I golf long enough to shoot my age.
  —*Golfers' Prayer*

You can talk to a slice, but a hook won't listen.
  —*Lee Trevino*

You drive for show but putt for dough.
  —*Bobby Locke*

Golf is ninety percent mental, the other half is skill.
  —*Yogi Berra*

Golf Jokes

The following golf jokes are a collection of ones usually told by golfers in the 19th hole:

Jonah, Moses, Jesus, and this older man were playing golf on this very difficult par three hole that had a lake in front of the green. Jonah hit his tee shot into the lake, but suddenly a great fish spit his ball onto the green 4-feet from the hole. Moses hit his tee shot toward the water, but suddenly the waters parted and the ball rolled to within 3-feet of the hole. Jesus hit his ball toward the water, but suddenly the ball seems to walk across the water to within 2-feet of the hole. Now this older man hit his ball toward the water, but suddenly a squirrel ran out of the woods, grabbed the ball into his mouth and started running away, but suddenly an eagle flew down and grabbed the squirrel and flew over the green, dropped the squirrel, the squirrel hit the green, the ball came out of his mouth and rolled into the hole. Jesus turned and said, "Nice shot, dad."

St. Peter was reviewing his tabloid on this man's earthly life that had just entered heaven. "You lived an outstanding Christian life while on earth. You committed only one sin. It says here in your tabloid that you once cursed while playing golf. Tell me about it for I also love to play golf." The golfer explained that all he had to do was par the last hole and he would win his club championship. His tee shot hit a tree branch that was hanging over the fairway and his ball bounced into the rough. "This made you curse?" asked St. Peter. "No!" the golfer replied. "I still thought that I could hit my 4-wood out of the rough, clear the sand bunker guarding the green, and still par the hole. My 4-wood shot hit above the bunker but took a bad bounce back into the bunker." "This probably caused you to curse," remarked St. Peter. "No! I felt like I still had a chance for a par because I had been practicing my bunker shots for months. When I arrived at the sand bunker, someone had forgotten to rake the sand and my ball was in a deep foot-print." "Obviously, you cursed," replied St. Peter who was now feeling sympathy for a fellow golfer. "No! I felt if I could open the clubface of my sand wedge and swing hard, I could clear the high ridge of the bunker and roll the ball close enough to sink my putt for a par. I dug into the sand with my feet, took a mighty swing. The ball barely cleared the lip of the bunker, and rolled to within 6-inches of the hole." St. Peter in amazement remarked, "You didn't miss that damn putt, did you?"

Jesus, who was disguised as an ordinary man, was playing golf on this very difficult par 3-hole with a lake in front of the green. Jesus asked his caddy what iron he should hit. The caddy suggested a 3-iron. Jesus disagreed and wanted a 6-iron. The caddy's rebuttal was that only Arnold Palmer could hit a 6-iron over that water.

Jesus insisted on a 6-iron and proceeded to hit his 6-iron into the water. Jesus, not wanting to lose his golf ball, walked out onto the water to retrieve it. Some other golfers saw Jesus walking on the water and asked his caddy if this man thought he was Jesus Christ. "No", remarked his caddy, "He thinks he is Arnold Palmer."

A disgusted golfer was at the driving range practicing, trying to put some order into a terribly erratic swing. He noticed a man who had a giant gorilla hitting golf balls. The gorilla would assume his stance, grunt loudly, and crush the ball 500 yards straight down the middle. He asked the man if he could use his pet gorilla as his partner to beat these two guys who were always beating him out of his money on golf bets. The owner agreed, and the anxiously inspired golfer showed up the next day with a new bet for his hesitant friends. The first hole was a 500-yard straight par-five. The three golfers all hit their drives 240 yards into the fairway. The gorilla assumed his stance, grunted loudly, and hit his ball 500 yards straight onto the green 3-feet from the hole. A big smile came across his playing partner's face. He started talking trash to his opponents. "I've got you now." "I'm going to get my money back." The three golfers all made par on the hole. The gorilla lined up his 3-foot double eagle putt, grunted loudly, and hit his putt 500 yards straight into the woods.

This avid golfer and his wife were surveying his terrible lie. His second shot required him to hit a 1-iron through a very small opening between two large trees. After careful study he decided to chip out of the trees and play it safe. His wife disagreed with his decision and encouraged him to go for the green in two by hitting a perfectly controlled 1-iron shot. Reluctantly, he agreed to try this very risky shot. His shot hit the tree and ricocheted backward, hitting his wife in the head and killing her instantly. A week later he was playing golf with his best friend, and as fate would have it, his ball again landed in the same position. His friend encouraged him to try his 1-iron shot between the trees. He snapped back, "The last time I had this shot I was playing with my dear wife, and I boggied the hole."

This exhausted golfer returned home after a long day on the course. His wife asked him why he was so exhausted. "My best friend Joe died of a heart attack on the third hole," was his reply. "Oh my! What did you do?" she asked. "I hit my ball and drug Joe for 15 holes," was his reply, "and I'm exhausted."

Joe and Bill were avid golfing buddies and they wanted to know if there were golf courses in heaven. Joe died and went to heaven. Upon arriving in heaven, he convinced St. Peter to allow him to return to earth and tell his life-long friend that there were beautiful golf courses in heaven. He appeared to Bill and informed him that there were beautiful golf courses in heaven, and that Bill had a tee time on one of them in the morning.

This foursome was playing their daily round of golf when suddenly a funeral procession started passing by. Tom took off his golf hat and put it over his heart. His friends were amazed that Tom would show such respect for an individual. When asked why he performed such a noble gesture, Tom commented that they had been married for 30 years and he felt like it was the proper thing to do.

A pro challenged a rich 20-handicapper to a wager in golf. The rich man accepted provided he would get two "got-you's" in the 18-hole match. On the first hole the pro was carefully lining up his putt, and on his back swing the rich man grabbed him in the buttocks and yelled "got -you." The pro knocked his putt off the green. After completing the 18-hole match, the pro was seen paying off his very sizeable wager to the rich man. Another golfer asked the pro why he was paying off a 20-handicapper since he was a much better player than he. The pro's only response was, "Have you ever tried to swing at a golf ball when someone has another "got-you" left?"

One beautiful Sunday a preacher, who was also an avid golfer, decided to call in sick so he could go play golf in this town where no one would recognize him. During the round he hit a 2-iron, 215 yards over water, into the cup for his first hole-in-one. St. Peter and God were looking down from heaven and witnessed this miraculous shot. St. Peter asked God why he allowed him to make a shot like that, especially since he skipped church. God said, "Who is he going to tell?"

These two golfers were vehemently complaining to the pro about the unusually slow play of the twosome that played in front of them. After listening to their insulting remarks about the slow twosome, the pro explained that the reason they took extra time to play was because they were blind. Still mad, one of the golfers angrily suggested to the pro, "Then you should have given them a tee time at night."

This single golfer was placed with this threesome, and as an icebreaker he asked the three large golfers if they wanted to hear an aggie joke. One of the large golfers quickly explained that all three of them had graduated from A&M and played tackle on the football team, and was he sure he wanted to tell that aggie joke? "No", he replied, "I don't want to have to repeat it three times."

This golfer, who was an avid golfer, had been marooned on this deserted island for two years. One day, while sitting on the beach, a beautiful woman came walking out of the ocean with a tight fitting wet suit on. The ecstatic golfer jumped up and ran down to meet her. He told her of his long isolated ordeal. She said, "I bet you would like a good ham sandwich," and unzipped a small compartment in her wet suit and removed the sandwich. "Yes, thank you," was his reply. Then she said, "I bet you would also like a bottle of wine," as she unzipped another compartment in her wet suit. "Yes, thank you," he graciously answered. Then the beautiful woman said, "I bet you would like to play around," as she unzipped her front zipper, revealing her cleavage. The excited golfer responded, "You mean you have some golf clubs in there?"

This beginning golfer was hitting bad shots during the round. He asked his caddy, "Why do you keep looking at your watch?" "It isn't a watch, sir, it's a compass," responded the caddy.

This couple was arguing when the wife remarked, "You think so much of your old golf game that you don't even remember when we got married." "Of course I do, my dear, it was the day I sank a 3-iron shot for an eagle on the seventeenth hole to beat Bill," he proudly recalled.

This golfer, who was not very good, hired a caddy to help him around the course. The more holes he played, the worse he got, and the more the caddy got fed-up watching his terrible attempt to play this great game. Finally, the two reached the eighteenth hole. The caddy grunted a sigh of relief. The golfer, smiling all over his face, turned to the caddy and said, "You perhaps won't believe this but I once made this hole in one." The caddy, exhausted from watching this spectacle, said, "Stroke or day, sir?"

This golfer died and unfortunately had a date with the devil. The devil welcomed him to hell, and began showing him some beautiful golf clubs. "Take your pick," replied the devil. The golfer chose the best set. The devil then gave him a new pair of golf shoes and took him to the most beautiful golf course one could imagine. The golfer thought that if hell were like this, then his future would be all right. He asked the devil for a dozen Titlest golf balls to go along with his beautiful clubs. "I am sorry," replied the devil, "that's the heck of it—there are no balls."

Did you hear about the bridegroom walking up to the altar with his golf clubs slung over his shoulders, and impatiently confronted the preacher, "Well, this is not going to take all day, is it?"

Two psychiatrists were playing a round of golf and one topped his shot and saw it roll into the lake. He muttered "Nuts". "Don't start talking shop," said his companion.

A golfer and his wife were often quarreling because he spent so much time at golf and so little time at home. One day, the argument got particularly heated and finally, in desperation, the husband shouted, "For goodness sake, woman, shut up! You are driving me out of my mind." "That, my dear," said the wife sweetly, "would hardly be a drive; it would be a short putt."

"Why do you play so much golf?" his wife angrily asked. "To keep fit, my dear," was his reply. "Fit for what?" she snapped back. "Why, to play more golf," was his logical rebuttal.

This horrible golfer took four mighty swings at the ball and each time sent a sizeable clump of earth skywards. Two worms were watching these antics, and one fearfully said to the other, "Let's get on top of the ball before this fellow kills us!"

Two golfers were about to drive off the fifth hole when, much to their surprise, a beautiful woman scantily dressed, leapt from the bushes at one side of the fairway, crossed it, and disappeared into the bushes on the other side. A few moments later a man in a white coat ran across the fairway chasing after the woman. Then another man in a white coat came bolting out of the woods following after them. Then another man, again wearing a white coat, came struggling behind carrying a huge bucket of sand in his right hand. This proved too much for the golfers, who decided to stop the next person and find out what was happening. "Well," replied the next breathless individual, "the young lady comes from a mental home just down the road. She has sudden fits where she tears off most of her clothes, climbs from the window, and runs away. The gentlemen in white coats are attendants at the Home. We have to catch her and bring her back." One of the golfers asked, "What is the significance of the sand in the bucket." "Oh," "That's old Bob. He caught her last time, and the bucket of sand is his handicap," explained the attendant.

This golfer was asked why he always wore two pairs of pants while playing golf. "Because he might get a "hole-in-one", was his logical reply.

"This can't be my ball, caddy," said the 20-handicapper, "It looks too old." "Well, sir" replied the caddy, "Don't forget, it's been a long time since we started."

St. Peter wanted to play golf so he asked Albert Einstein to help him by filling in for him at the pearly gates and welcome the new arrivals to heaven. Albert agreed, and asked the first person what was his I.Q. The man responded that it was 190. Albert excitedly welcomed him into heaven and remarked that they could discuss the theory of relativity. He asked the second man what was his I.Q. The man responded that it was 140. Albert welcomed him in and said that he looked forward to discussing medicine with him. Einstein asked the third man what was his I.Q. The third man responded that it was 80. Einstein's only remark was, "How is your golf game?"

This golfer made a six on the hole. He told his caddy that he made a five. The caddy wrote down a four. The second caddy asked him why he wrote down the wrong score. "He wanted to help him with his "lie" was his subordinate reply.

The wife of an avid golfer found some ladies panties in her husband's clothes drawer and immediately suspected that he was having an affair with another woman. She called his best golfing friend John, and relayed her suspicions about him having an affair with another woman. John, very tactfully assured her that her husband was not having an affair with another woman. He said, "Her husband would do anything to hit from the ladies tees."

This golfer showed up to play golf with his regular foursome wearing a corset. One of his friends asked if he had hurt his back. He replied that his back was not hurt and that he had never had back problems in his life. "Then why are you wearing the corset?" asked his puzzled friend. "You would wear one too if your wife found the corset under the front seat of your car," was his logical reply.

A rich old man after his death left 100 million dollars to either the Catholic Church in the Vatican or to the Jewish Church in Israel. In his will he stipulated that the money would go to the winner of a golf match between church representatives from each religion. The Pope asked if there were any cardinals that were good enough to represent their church. The cardinals reported that Jack Nicklaus was a devout catholic, and if the Pope would make him a cardinal then he would surely win the 100 million. Jack Nicklaus graciously consented to play the match for his church. After the golf match Jack Nicklaus reported to the Pope. The Pope asked Cardinal Nicklaus how the match ended. Cardinal Nicklaus said that he had some good news and some bad news. The good news was that he played the best round of his life. Every drive was down the middle; he hit every green in regulation; and made almost every putt he had. However, the bad news is that Rabbi Woods beat him by three shots.

There was a long line of new arrivals waiting to get into heaven to talk to St. Peter concerning their rewards for their good and just life while on earth. The people in the back of the line kept hearing loud cheering and celebrations from the people at the front of the line. Finally, one of people in the rear curiosity got the best of him and he ran up to the front of line to see what all the cheering was about. He returned to the back of the line with a big smile on his face. One of the anxious arrivals asked, "What was going on?" His relieved reply was, "He is not going to count our ugly golf superlatives from hitting bad shots."

This sixty-year-old man was playing golf with his sixty-year-old wife, when he sliced his ball deep into the woods where his ball hit a leprechaun in the head knocking him unconscious. The leprechaun had to grant the couple one wish each for they had captured him. The lady wished she could travel free to anyplace in the world. Zap! She received a handful of airline tickets to every continent on earth. The 60 year old man wished he would be given a beautiful woman, with a 4 handicap, and thirty years younger. Zap! The man became 90 years old.

Golf Anecdotes about My Friend Bob

The following are a collection of funny anecdotes about my friend Bob and our 40 years of playing golf together. Maybe you can recognize your golfing friends in these anecdotes. Hopefully, they will help you remember all the good times you have had while playing this "wild and crazy" game.

The old saying, "If I didn't have any bad luck, I wouldn't have any luck at all," really applies to my friend Bob. The laws of physics that govern the universe do not work the same for Bob as they do for normal human beings. I have never seen a man's golf ball take such bad bounces, land in such precarious positions, cause so much harm, or do so many unnatural things as Bob's. Our club members all gather around to watch with anticipation about what is going to happen on his next swing. My friend Bob is "unlucky." Read on and see if you don't agree.

Bob and I were playing this very difficult par three hole that had water on three sides of the green, with a 40-foot high cliff extending from the tee box to the right side of the green. Bob sliced his tee shot and the ball landed on top of the cliff about two feet from the edge of the 40-foot drop into a lake below. Bob had to assume his stance with his feet dangerously close to the watery abyss below. After assuming his stance, a confident look came across his face, for he figured he could still beat me on the hole and win our fifty-cent wager. I was hitting three from the drop area, since my ball failed to clear the icy waters below. Bob carefully entrenched his spikes into the edge of the cliff. As he shifted his weight backward in his back swing, the edge of the cliff collapsed. Bob's legs immediately fell off the cliff, causing him to drop to his elbows desperately grasping the edge of the cliff for his survival. From where I was standing I could see the panic in his eyes. I rushed to help my terrorized friend, but was a fraction of a second too late. I heard him splash into the cold water below as he screamed the word describing a person's fecal-end products. Somehow in his struggle to cling to the cliff he must have hit his ball with his club for the ball also fell from the cliff landing in the water only a few inches from my "very-infuriated" friend. By the way, Bob made a triple-boggy; I made a double-boggy and won fifty cents.

Bob and I had a one-stroke advantage, with one hole to play, to win this two-man, low-ball, golf tournament. The last hole was a par-five with a large bunker guarding the dogleg in the fairway. Bob crushed his drive, which carried over the bunker and rolled to within an iron shot of the green. My tee ball buried in the sand bunker. Our opponents hit their shots short of the bunker. Jubilantly, we jumped into our golf cart, each praising Bob's great drive, and smelling victory. We recklessly started driving our golf cart toward our golf shots as Bob simultaneously started to take a sip of pop from a straw in his cup. The cart hit a large hole in the cart path, sending the straw up Bob's nose and severing his nasal artery. His nose bled so profusely that my friend became sick and passed-out. My wife took him to the pro shop for first-aid, while I finished the last hole to complete the tournament. When I arrived at the pro shop to check on my friend, he asked excitedly, "What happened on the last hole?" In a tone of complete disgust, I had to report, " I boggied the hole, our opponents birdied the hole, and we finished second in the tournament."

Bob and I were playing partners competing in a two-man, low-ball, tournament. We were one-shot behind with one hole to play. Bob sliced his tee shot into some tall oak trees. As we surveyed his second shot, we both came to the same conclusion that he should select his driver and blast his ball between two large oak trees and maybe reach the green on this par 5 hole. As Bob was preparing to hit his shot, I kept encouraging him with positive superlatives such as, "You can do it", "grip it and rip it", and "sacrifice your body for the team."

I could see my encouragement was working, for adrenaline was now pouring into Bob's excited body. He started taking deep, quick, breaths. His blood pressure was rising, and his heart rate was nearing the fibrillation rate. I've never seen any golfer more ready to hit his shot. With all the strength Bob could muster, he crushed the ball as hard as he could. The ball solidly hit the tree, ricocheted backward toward Bob, hitting him in his male organ of copulation. Bob immediately doubled up and fell screaming to the ground. He was in such pain and agony that we had to put him in a golf cart, still doubled-up and vomiting, and carry him to the hospital, thus forfeiting the tournament.

Bob and I arrived at the golf course to play in this very prestigious tournament. Bob noticed that his golf shoes were worn and ragged and needed to be replaced. He purchased a pair of golf shoes that cost him $180. Bob was very proud of these fine waterproof, flexible leather shoes, in which the spikes would never have to be replaced. It was by far the best pair of golf shoes that he had ever owned. He asked the pro to also throw in this fancy large umbrella, because it was clouding up and it might rain during his round. As fate would have it, the heavens opened up and it started raining along with brilliant flashes of lighting hitting all around. All the golfers immediately took to covered shelter. Bob started toward the covered shelter when a bolt of lightening hit his umbrella. The lightning traveled through his body and came out of his toe, blowing a large hole in his fancy new shoes. Bob was knocked to the ground. Stunned and unable to walk, Bob desperately started crawling as fast as he could through the mud and water toward shelter, still holding on to his charred umbrella. All the golfers under the shelter saw the panic in his eyes and started yelling encouragements such as "faster, hurry, you can make it." There is some good news and some bad news concerning this incident. Bob made it and recovered from his burns. However, the shoes were not guaranteed against lightning strikes, and Bob lost his $180 plus a new $40 umbrella.

Bob and I were sitting at an outside table at the golf club discussing what a terrible round we just completed. It was one of those rounds where nothing went right. Our shots hit trees, we had terrible lies, and our putts lipped out. We were really crying about our bad luck. Suddenly, a bird flew over Bob and deposited his waste on him. Bob just looked up toward heaven and remarked, "God, your creatures "sing" for other people."

Bob always carries a cellular phone with him while he plays golf. His boss still thinks he is working selling his products throughout the city. Every time his boss calls we have to be very quiet in order to protect his job. During one round Bob's phone rang several times, interrupting his play. Bob commented that he couldn't wait until he could retire. I said, "Bob what would you do differently?" "You already play golf six days a week." Bob snapped back, "I would leave this dang phone at home."

I hit one of my best drives of my life straight down the middle. I turned to Bob and confidently remarked, "Catch that one, Alice." Bob crushed his drive, and his ball flew past mine in the air. Bob commented, "That's a Linda Ronstadt drive." I asked, "What kind of drive is that?" Bob egotistically said, "It blew by-you."

Bob and I were invited to play golf on the most difficult golf course in America. Our host kept telling us how difficult this course is to play. After listening to his horror stories about how we would not be able to break 90, we developed the dry heaves before we even arrived at the course. On the first hole, Bob teed up his ball, assumed his stance and grip, took a mighty swing, and completely missed the ball. Bob only comment was, "You're right; this is a tough course."

Bob and I were playing this very long and difficult par three hole. We both hit two-iron right at the flag. The hole had a large undulation in the green, which prohibited us from seeing the cup. When we arrived at the green, we saw only one ball about two-feet from the hole. I marked the ball with a coin. We thought Bob's ball must have gone over the green. After searching, Bob said maybe it went into the hole. He looked into the hole and started yelling, "It is in the hole; I made my first hole-in-one!" I've never seen a more happy man. As I was replacing my ball on my mark, I realized that this ball was Bob's ball. I started yelling, "I made the hole-in-one." I had marked Bob's ball, while my ball was the one in the hole. By the way, Bob missed his two-foot putt.

I was caddying for Bob as he was playing in his first professional tournament, and struggling to make the 36-hole cut. He had to sink a thirty-foot putt for a par on the last hole to have a chance to make the cut. When Bob struck his putt, the ball started breaking toward the hole. I also realized that I had a big problem. My responsibility was to remove the flagstick, but it was jammed hard into the hole. As the putt got closer to the hole I began to panic. I finally gave the stick one last hard pull, which caused the metal cylinder in the hole to come up above the ground. Bob's ball struck the metal cylinder and ricocheted to the left. Bob missed the cut, and didn't speak to me on the return trip home.

Bob was beating me like a drum in our golf round. I knew desperate measures had to be taken in order for me to stand a chance against this birdie machine. I made the comment that he was sure swinging good today. I asked, "Do you pronate your wrist at contact with the ball, or does your wrist supinate at ball contact?" A confused look came across Bob's face, and he remarked, "I really don't know." On his next shot he hooked his tee shot into the water. He looked disgustedly at me and commented, "I guess I pronate."

The weather turned bad while Bob and I were playing golf. It started raining and lightning, so Bob ran as fast as he could for shelter. I said to him, "I guess you have learned your lesson about the dangers of being hit by lightning." Bob, who was once hit by lightning, said, "The lesson I have learned from my terrifying experience is, "If God wants to play through, you let him play through."

Bob had a one-stroke advantage, putting on the final hole, for our club championship. All Bob had to do was two-putt from 40-feet to win the club tournament. His first putt rolled to within one-foot of the hole. Bob decided to mark his ball with a coin in order not to stand in his opponents' line. Bob tapped the coin down with his putter, the coin stuck to the bottom of his putter, and Bob walked away not knowing what had happened. When he tried to remark his ball, he realized what had happened, accepted his two-stroke penalty, and again came in second in the club championship.

Bob and I were tied for our club championship. We were playing as if we were in mortal combat. My tee shot landed in a hole that was located under a large oak tree. I asked Bob if a burrowing animal made the hole. If so, it would give me a free drop. "No way," Bob quickly responded. I snapped back, "I bet that hole was made by an armadillo." Our pro quickly stepped in and made the ruling that the hole was made by a washout and no free drop would be allowed. I sadly reached into the hole to retrieve my ball, when suddenly an armadillo ran out. I got a free drop and birdied the hole. By the way, Bob finished second in the club championship again.

Bob ripped his tee shot straight down the middle. "Bob yelled S-S." I asked, "What does "S-S" mean?" Bob said, "It means Smoke City." To this day I have never corrected him concerning his faulty spelling.

Our golfing gang always meets in the 19th hole to go over the day's round. The winners were bragging about their great shots. The losers were complaining about how the golf God had forsaken them when they needed him. Bob's comment about his round was the best of the day. He said, "The only two good balls I hit all day were when I stepped on the rake in the sand trap."

Bob had this very difficult iron shot over a sand trap. The pin was located close to the trap, and the green slanted downward toward the hole. It would take a miracle to stop his ball close to the hole. Bob's shot hit short of the hole, took the bit, ran slowly down the undulation, and ended up close to the hole. Bob remarked, "That shot landed like a butterfly with sore feet."

Bob took a mighty swing with his driver, but the ball barely left the tee box. Bob's only comment about this poorly hit shot was, "I hit that drive with the Ladies Home Journal." I commented, "It must have been with the panty-hose section of the magazine."

Bob was giving this beginner a golf lesson. The beginner asked Bob, "What was wrong with his swing?" Bob answered, "You are standing too close to the ball—after you hit it."

Bob commented on his round in which he had hit several balls into water hazards, "Today, I hit so many balls into the water; I'm going to have to regrip my ball retriever."

Bob, trying to avoid the water hazard on the left, sliced his ball into the deep rough on the right. Bob described this poorly hit shot as a "Rush Limbaugh" shot. "What kind of shot is that?' I asked. "Too far to the **"right,"** was his reply? I responded, "That's better than hitting a Bill Clinton shot". "You know, too far to the **"left"** and **"lost."**

Bob and I were playing in this golf tournament and needed a par on the last hole to win. Bob was carefully surveying his 150-yard shot to the green, while pondering what club he should select for this pressure shot. Confused, Bob turned to me and asked, "Partner, should I hit a "fat" six-iron, or a "bladed" eight-iron?" I quickly responded, "Why don't you hit a "smooth" seven-iron?" He said, "I don't have that shot."

Bob once had this 6-foot putt for a birdie to win this tournament. After he had carefully surveyed his putt from every conceivable angle, he proceeded to knock his ball about 12-feet past the hole. He angrily turned and commented, "I just had a **"focal dystonia"**. "What's a "focal dystonia?" I asked. "It's the medical term for a "brain cramp," was his disheartened reply.

Bob needed to make this 10-foot putt to win his match. He stroked his putt; the ball caught the lip of the cup, made a complete circle around the cup, and barely fell in. I sarcastically commented that he was sure lucky that the ball fell into the hole. He confidently said, "No, he wasn't lucky." "His ball just wanted to take a "victory lap" before falling in."

After missing a short putt, Bob angrily tossed his putter across the green. I commented that a good golfer must remain even-tempered if he is going to be successful in golf. Bob snapped back that his wife would be a great golfer. "How is that?" I remarked. "Because she is "always" mad," was his pugnacious reply.

Bob, playing this long par five hole, hooked his tee shot into the rough on the **left.** He sliced his second shot across the fairway into the rough on the **right.** He hooked his third shot back across the fairway into the rough on the **left.** He then sliced his fourth shot into the rough to the **right** of the green. Bob disgustedly remarked, "I'm playing Army golf." "What kind of golf is Army golf?" I asked. "You know, left, right, left, right," was his angry response.

Bob hit a horrible drive and in utter disgust proclaimed that he hated golf, hated the man who invented golf, and hated everything that is associated with golf, however, he continued, it was the only thing he enjoyed doing.

Bob and I were playing in a two-man scramble golf tournament, and we each purchased a putting mulligan. During the tournament Bob missed a short putt, so I quickly reminded him that he had a second chance to putt again by using his mulligan. His response was that he was putting so bad that he had to use his mulligan while practicing on the putting green.

Bob's long putt came to rest hanging on the lip of the cup; Bob in disgust proclaimed, "Well at least the ball's shadow fell into the cup."

Bob topped his drive and the ball rolled about 100 yards into the rough. "I just hit a Frank Shorter drive", Bob screamed. What is a Frank Shorter drive? I asked. "It is a cross country runner", was his disgusted reply.

Bob once hit three balls into the lake. Being very depressed Bob remarked that he was going to jump into the lake and drown himself. I commented that from the way you are swinging at the ball I don't think you can keep your head down that long.

Bob was giving a playing lesson to one of his students when the student asked, "How do you like my game?" Bob remarked, "Very good, however, I prefer golf."

Bob once asked me if I thought he could hit a 5-iron 200 yards to the green. Thinking that he was grading his paper too high I remarked, "eventually."

Golfer's Prayer

Lord Jesus, in the game of life as in the game of golf, help me to be a good sport. I don't ask for a convenient starting time. Put me anywhere on the course where you need me. I only ask that you help me to give 100 percent of all that I have.

If you place me in the thick roughs or deep sand traps I will thank you for the compliment. Help me to remember that you never send a player more trouble than he can handle.

Help me, oh Lord, to accept the weird bounces as part of the game. I don't want to gripe about the grain of the green, or the lie of the ball. May I always play the game the right way no matter what others do. Show me the rules so I'll be sure to play by the Book.

Finally, Lord, if the natural turn of events go against me and I have to closet my clubs for sickness or old age, please help me to accept my new role. Keep me from whimpering about unfairness or grumbling about the brevity of time.

When I finish the 18th hole I ask for no laurels or spectators. But as I walk away give me the assurance that I fought a good fight and finished the course and didn't let You down.

Amen

M. Dean Register, Th.D

Skills Test

Beginning, Intermediate, and Advanced Golf Skills Test

Putting	100	95	90	85	80	75	70
3 feet							
Beg.	5/5	4/5	3/5		2/5		1/5
Int.	5/5		4/5	3/5		2/5	1/5
Adv.	5/5		4/5		3/5		2/5
10 feet							
Beg.	4/5	3/5	2/5	1/5	2p 5/5	2p less than 5/5	
Int.	5/5	4/5	3/5	2/5	1/5		0/5
Adv.	5/5	4/5	3/5	2/5		1/5	0/5
20 feet (2 putt)							
Beg.	5/5	4/5	3/5		2/5		1/5
Int.	5/5		4/5	3/5		2/5	0/5
Adv.	5/5			4/5	3/5		2/5

3 ft. ___ + 10 ft. ___ + 20 ft. ___ = ___ /3 = ____

Chipping

Chip from 30' to a 3' radius circle from 2' off the green

	100	95	90	85	80	75	70
Beg.	5/5	4/5	3/5	2/5	1/5		0/5
Int.	5/5	4/5	3/5		2/5	1/5	0/5
Adv.	5/5	4/5		3/5		2/5	0/5

= _____

Pitching

Pitch to a 5' radius circle from 5 yards off the green

	100	95	90	85	80	75	70
Beg.	5/5	4/5	3/5	2/5	1/5		0/5
Int/Adv.	5/5	4/5	3/5		2/5	1/5	0/5

= _____

Swing fundamentals

Have students hit 3 shots and count the best 2. (-10 for each area)

	swing 1	swing 2	swing 3
Set up	_____	_____	_____
Posture	_____	_____	_____
Balance	_____	_____	_____

Posture ___ + ___ /2 = _____

Putting ____ + chipping ____ + pitching ___ + swing ___ /4 = _____
Name _____ sec. _____ time _____ skills grade

GLOSSARY

Ace: A hole completed in one stroke.

Address: The process that a player goes through in positioning himself and the club or a stroke.

Approach shot: A full stroke played to the putting green, usually made with a medium or short iron.

Apron: The bordering grass around the green, not as short as the green but usually shorter than the fairway. Sometimes called the "fringe".

Away: The ball deemed farthest from the hole, to be played first.

Back Door: A description for a putt which rolls around the cup and falls in from the rear.

Back Nine: The second nine holes of an eighteen-hole golf course.

Backspin: A reverse spin imparted to the ball, which causes it to stop quickly upon landing.

Banana Ball: A slang term for a shot, which curves wildly from left to right.

Best Ball: A match in which one golfer plays against the better ball of two players or the best ball of three players.

Birdie: A score of one stroke under par for a hole.

Bite: Backspin imparted to the ball, which makes it stop abruptly.

Blade: Description of a putter with a thin head.

Bogey: A score of one stroke over par on a hole.

Brassie: The #2 wood. Seldom included in a matched set of clubs today.

Break of Green: The slant or the slope of the green, sometimes called "borrow," when considering the amount of curve to allow for.

Bunker: A hazard or a depressed area filled with sand. In common usage called a sand trap.

Caddie: Someone who carries a player's clubs. A caddie may give advice to the player.

Carry: The distance that a ball travels in the air before striking the ground.

Casual Water:	An accumulation of water which is temporary. Not considered a water hazard.
Chip Shot:	A short and usually low-trajectory shot played to the green.
Closed Face:	One in which the face of the club points to the left of the intended line of flight.
Closed Stance:	The left foot is closer to the intended line of flight than the right foot.
Clubface:	The normal striking surface of the head of the club.
Course Rating:	The difficulty rating of a course assigned by a committee which uses guidelines provided by the United States Golf Association.
Couey Corollary:	Named for Dick Couey who hated to, and usually missed, short putts. His fellow players allowed him to pick up short putts that were within, or even touched, the putter's grip.
Cup:	The metal lining of the hole on the putting green. It is 4 1/4" in diameter and at least 4" deep.
Cut Shot:	A stroke, which gives the ball a clockwise spin and causes it to curve from left to right.
Divot:	A piece of turf which is displaced by a player's club. It should be replaced and patted down, or filled in with sand and seed.
Dogleg:	A hole with a fairway, which bends to the right or to the left.
Dormie:	A situation in match play in which a player or a team is leading by as many holes as there are holes remaining.
Double Bogey:	A score of two strokes over par on a hole.
Double Eagle:	A score of three strokes under par on a hole.
Down:	The number of holes a player or a side is behind in a match.
Draw:	A shot which curves slightly to the left.
Drive:	A shot made from the teeing ground.
Driver:	The #1 wood or metal club.
Dub:	A poorly hit shot.
Duffer:	A poor golfer. Also sometimes called a "hacker."
Eagle:	A score of two strokes under par on a hole.
Explosion Shot:	A shot from a sand bunker in which the club head slides under the ball and displaces a fairly large amount of sand.
Fade:	A shot which curves slightly to the right.
Fairway:	The mowed area of the golf course between the teeing ground and the putting green.

Fat Shot:	A stroke in which the ground is struck before the ball.
Flag or flagstick:	The movable pole in the hole with a flag attached to the top. Also called the pin.
Flat Swing:	A swing which is less upright and more shallow than the normal swing.
Flight:	The path that the ball takes in the air; or a division of players in a tournament according to playing ability.
Follow-Through:	The part of the swing after the clubface has contacted the ball.
Fore:	A warning which is shouted to anyone in danger of being hit by a golf ball.
Foursome:	The common term for four players playing in a group.
Forward Press:	A slight movement toward the target of some part of the body prior to the backswing.
Frog Hair:	Same as apron.
Gimmie:	A slang expression for a conceded putt in match plays.
Grain:	The direction in which flat-lying grass grows on a putting green.
Grip:	The upper portion of the club shaft. Also the player's grasp of the club.
Gross Score:	The player's actual score on a hole or a round, with no handicap strokes deducted.
Ground:	Touching the ground with the sole of the club at address. This is not allowed in a hazard.
Ground Under Repair:	Designated areas on a golf course, which allow for free drop outside those areas.
Halved:	A term used to designate a tied hole in match play.
Handicap:	A number which indicates a golfer's skill. It is based upon the difference between the actual scores a player shoots and the course ratings of the courses on which the scores were made. It provides a way for players of different abilities to play on a fairly equal basis.
Hazard:	According to the United States Golf Association rules, a designation for a bunker, sand trap, water area, or water hazard.
Head:	The striking part of the club at the lower end of the shaft.
Heeled Shot:	A shot hit near or off the portion of the club that attaches to the shaft.
High Side:	The area above the hole on a sloping green.
Hole Out:	To stroke the ball into the cup.
Honor:	The privilege of shooting first from the teeing ground.

Hood:	A closed clubface. Tilting the top edge of the club forward, thus decreasing the loft.
Hook:	A shot which curves in flight from right to left.
Hosel:	The extension of the head of the club into which the shaft fits.
In:	The designation on a score card for the second nine holes of an eighteen-hole course.
Inside-Out:	The club head moves across the intended line of flight from left to right during impact.
Interlock Grip:	A type of grip in which the left forefinger and right little finger are intertwined.
LPGA:	The Ladies Professional Golf Association.
Lag:	Putting with the intention of ending close to the hole.
Lateral Water Hazard:	A water hazard, which runs parallel or almost parallel to the line of play on a hole.
Lie:	The position of the ball on the course. Also refers to the angle formed by the sole of the club and the shaft.
Links:	A term, which refers to, that which is built over sandy soil deposited by ocean tides ("linked to the seas"). Today a term used synonymously with golf course.
Lip:	The edge of the hole. Also a putt which rims the hole but does not go in.
Loft of the Club:	The backward slant or angle of the clubface. Also, to cause the ball to rise into the air.
Loose Impediment:	A natural object not fixed or growing, such as pebbles, leaves, and twigs.
Low Side:	The area below the hole on a slanted green.
Mashie:	A hickory-shafted iron club approximately like the current #5 iron.
Match Play:	Competition based on the number of holes won or lost rather than on strokes.
Medal:	The lowest of all of the qualifying scores. The person shooting this score is the medalist.
Mulligan:	In friendly competition, an illegal second shot from the first tee if the first shot is a poor one. Named after a Canadian, Dr. David Mulligan.
Nassau:	A type of scoring in which three points is given: one for each nine holes and one for the eighteen holes.
Net Score:	The score for a hole or for a round after the player's handicap has been deducted from the gross score.

Niblick: A club somewhat like the current #9 iron.

Obstruction: Usually refers to anything on the course, which is artificial, whether fixed, or movable. See USGA rules for exceptions.

Open Face: The club head is aimed right of the intended line of flight.

Open Stance: The right foot is closer than the left foot to the intended line of flight.

Open Tournament: Competition which allows the entry of both amateurs and professionals.

Out of Bounds: An area usually marked by stakes, a fence, or a wall, which is outside of the course proper. Play in this area is prohibited.

Out: The designation for the first nine holes of an eighteen-hole course, or designating which golfer is away from the hole.

Outside-In: Movement of the club head from right to left across the intended line of flight.

Overlap or Overlapping: The grip in which the right little finger laps over the left forefinger.

Par: The score a skilled player is expected to move on a hole. This score allows for two putts.

PGA: The men's Professional Golf Association.

Pitch Shot: An approach shot with a high trajectory, which stops relatively fast after landing.

Play Through: An invitation given by slower players to let the group behind them go ahead.

Preferred Lie: An easing of the rules that permits the players to move the ball to a better position in the fairway when course conditions are poor. Also called "winter rules."

Provisional Ball: A second ball which is hit before a player looks for an original ball which might be lost or out of bounds.

Press: Using more force than necessary or attempting to stroke beyond one's own ability; or doubling the original bet in wagering for the remaining holes.

Pull Shot: A shot which travels on a fairly straight line to the left of the intended target.

Push: A shot which travels on a fairly straight line to the right of the intended target.

Putter: The least-lofted club, which is usually used only on the putting green.

Rough: An area which has fairly long grass. It is not considered fairway, hazard,

	or green.
Rub of the Green:	A term used for the situation in which a shot is stopped or deflected by an outside agency.
Sand Wedge:	A club with a heavy, wide sole that is designed principally to be used in sand bunkers.
Scotch Foursome:	Common term for a foursome in which two teams compete, each team using only one ball and hitting it alternately.
Scrambler:	A player who shows exceptional skills around the green after demonstrating loose play in getting there. In other words, a slang expression for a player who can get the ball up and in the hole from out of a garbage can.
Scratch Player:	A player who has a handicap of zero and who plays consistently close to par.
Shanking:	Hitting the ball with the neck of the club, making it travel in an oblique direction to the right.
Skying:	Hitting the ball high in the air only a short distance, when it was intended to travel much farther.
Slice:	A shot which curves sharply from left to right of the intended line of flight.
Sole:	The bottom of the club head.
Spoon:	The #3 wood.
Square Stance:	A stance in which a line drawn from the toe of the right foot to the toe of the left foot runs parallel to the line of flight.
Square Face:	The club head is aimed at the intended line of flight at the address.
Stiff:	A shot which finished very close to the flagstick.
Stroke Play:	Competition based upon the total strokes taken by a player or a side.
Sudden Death:	Extra holes played by players tied at the end of competition until a winner is determined.
Summer Rules:	The official rules of golf that require the player to play the ball as it lie.
Takeaway:	The initial part of the backswing.
Target Line:	The imaginary line which extends from the player's target back to, through, and beyond the ball.
Tee:	The small wooden peg from which the ball is played on the teeing ground.
Teeing Ground:	A rectangular area defined by markers, which is no more than two club lengths in depth. The first shot of every hole is played from here and is

commonly called the "tee".

Tee Markers: The markers placed on the teeing ground that designate the point from which play of the hole begins.

Texas Wedge: A slang term that refers to the putter when it is used for shots from off the putting green.

Through the Green: A designation for the whole area of the course except the teeing ground and the green of the hole being played, and including all hazards.

Tight Lie: A ball that is well down in the grass or very close to the surface being played.

Toed Shot: A shot that is struck on or near the toe of the club.

Topped Shot: A rolling or low bounding shot that is caused by striking the ball above its center of gravity.

Unplayable Lie: A ball (not in a water hazard) which is determined to be unplayable by its owner.

USGA: The United States Golf Association, the governing body of golf in the United States. Organized in 1894.

Waggle: Club head movement at the time of address and prior to the swing.

Whiff: A miss. A stroke in which no contact is made with the ball.

Winter Rules: A situation in which the course is not in top playable condition; therefore a player is allowed to improve the lie of his/her ball.